Naperville: 175 Years of Success

is dedicated to all supporters of commerce

who, through free trade, job creation,

community development and technological progress,

have transformed a pioneer outpost into

a vibrant city for all ages.

CommunityLink Publication
A publishing service of Craig Williams Creative, Inc.

	production		business development		administrative support
production manager	PAM KELLERMAN	director of sales operations	DEBBIE MOSS	administrative support	KATHY HAGENE
director of media & content	DIANA VAUGHN	vp of business development	GEORGE PRUDHOMME		CAROL SMITH
copywriter	STEPHANIE PENICK	business development	BONNIE EBERS	account support	TARA BOLINGER
copy editor	LAURA WILCOXEN	sales representative	MIKE RAFERT		TRICIA CANNEDY
proofreader	CHRISTINA REESE			human resources assistant	TERESA CRAIG
photography	KEITH COTTON		advertising		
	LISA LEHR				information technology
creative director	CRAIG WILLIAMS	director of advertising	MATT PRICE		
director of publication design	CLINT EILERTS	ad research	JOYCE PYATT	publishing systems coordinator	CHRISTOPHER MILLER
cover design	AMANDA WHITE	ad traffic	CAROL SMITH		executive leadership
lead design	CLINT EILERTS	ad design	JENNIFER CONWELL		
supporting design	PAM KELLERMAN		PAUL LILLY		
marketing design	ERIN GRAY		KELLY PICKETT	chairman and founder	CRAIG WILLIAMS
			ALLAN SIMPSON	chief financial officer	RHONDA HARSY
			BECKY TRAIL		
			KACEY WOLTERS		

This book is published by CommunityLink and distributed through the Naperville Area Chamber of Commerce. For advertising information or questions or comments about this book contact CommunityLink at (866) 381-9759 or by e-mail at info@communitylink.com

FOR ADDITIONAL INFORMATION Naperville Area Chamber of Commerce, 55 South Main Street, Suite 351, Naperville, IL 60540, (630) 355-4141, Fax (630) 355-8335, www.naperville.net

Printed in Hong Kong

ISBN 0-9770027-0-5

NAPERVILLE

175 YEARS OF SUCCESS

Written by Stephanie Penick

Photography by Keith Cotton

Photography by Lisa Lehr

Naperville Area
CHAMBER OF COMMERCE

Heritage • Unity • Vision

Naperville
1831-2006

175 Years
www.naper175.org

Naperville is exceptional, no question about it! What makes it so exceptional at 175 years is its enduring sense of community. And people make the community.

Looking way back, a different kind of community thrived here before Captain Joseph Naper and his brother John discovered this fertile land along the DuPage River. Local inhabitants in this region were Native Americans and mostly seasonal residents, who also appreciated and respected what this land had to offer.

The area began to develop in 1831 when, aboard a schooner named the Telegraph, the Naper brothers sailed the Great Lakes from Ashtabula, Ohio, to Fort Dearborn. They brought their families to settle here — two years before Fort Dearborn on Lake Michigan became known as Chicago.

By horseback and Conestoga wagons, settlers followed the Napers' pioneer spirit and began to embrace the immense potential of this stretch along the banks of the DuPage, just 28 miles west of Chicago.

The Napers built a saw mill at the base of where Mill Street ends. It was just up the river from Bailey Hobson's grist mill. Hobson's family earned the distinction of being the first settlers to live in DuPage County. The early settlers also designed roads and stage coach routes and welcomed schools and churches. Farms flourished. Free enterprise took hold.

In time, log cabins were replaced with larger homes made of timber, limestone and bricks. And Naperville became a city on March 17, 1890. Prosperity and progress have driven Naperville's standard of living ever since.

I'm lucky to have known many of the visionaries who followed their dreams here in the 20th century. I've watched our town grow from a small farming community to a thriving metropolis approaching 140,000 residents.

And today, the same can-do spirit of adventure draws families and businesses to invest and reinvest in Naperville.

I like to think of my personal story as an American Dream.

In 1939, when I was 2 years old, my parents discovered Naperville when the population was about 5,000. We moved out here from Chicago, and my dad worked as a welder for the railroad.

I'm the oldest of six children, and many of our childhood friends lived on farms — practically next door.

All the way through eighth grade, I attended Bronsonville School, a one-room schoolhouse on the north side of town. Then I went to the brand-new Naperville High School — now known as Naperville Central High School — as a freshman, and was a member of the first graduating class to go there all four years.

After graduation, I joined the Marines to serve my country, married Pat, and we began our family. Our three children and our six grandchildren also have witnessed many changes growing up in this great community.

In 1966, I landed a job on the Naperville Police force, where I served for 29 years.

I enjoyed the best beat in the city, patrolling the downtown business district. Kids called me "Officer Friendly," and my passion has always been to put smiles on their faces and show we care about them here in Naperville. We started safety programs in the schools that led to a special program and place just for kids called "Safety Town."

I was promoted from sergeant to lieutenant in 1986, a rank I kept until 1995, when I retired to become mayor of our ever-evolving city. At that time, the population was about 110,000 residents.

As we celebrate 175 years of triumphs, glories and challenges, I'm in my 10th year as mayor. We've made it our business to connect with all citizens and entrepreneurs. We've also worked to attract and retain leading technological and retail corporations.

But let me also credit the 39 mayors before me. Starting with Joe Naper, all the way through my immediate predecessor, Sam Macrane, every person who ever served in this leadership position brought a different style to the office. Yet every mayor and council made a difference.

As a career police officer, imagine the pride I feel knowing that during my time as mayor, Naperville has been recognized as the only community in the world with fully accredited police, fire and emergency communications departments, demonstrating the community's commitment to public safety.

Naperville offers excellent city services in both DuPage and Will counties, two great school districts and many private schools, more than 150 parks, three libraries, North Central College and extensions of other colleges, worship opportunities in many faiths, an active chamber of commerce, and state-of-the-art health care. In fact, Edward Hospital, our community health center, is our largest employer.

Looking back, I see how fortunate I've been to personally know many generous residents who promoted and funded our dreams, helping to establish traditions.

And we enjoy traditions. With roots back to 1859, our Municipal Band performs summer concerts in Central Park. Our city displays lasting patriotism with memorials to veterans and annual parades to remember those who died for our freedom.

We've built natural treasures like Centennial Beach stone-by-stone and the Riverwalk brick-by-brick right in the heart of downtown. And we created an accredited outdoor 19th-century history museum called Naper Settlement to celebrate our rich history every day.

Add the Century Walk, the DuPage Children's Museum and performances at North Central College's Pfeiffer Hall, and our culture rivals much larger cities. Yet I like to think our community spirit and quality of life resemble a small town.

Our annual festivals and special celebrations are charitable. Our music programs and sports teams include champions.

We pride ourselves on a thriving economy and a historic downtown and look forward to all the plans for our south side and growing to 160,000 residents.

Our greeter programs, newcomers groups, service clubs and homeowners associations will continue to connect us all.

Just when you think "How can Naperville be any better?" some enthusiastic organization pitches in. Or a volunteer group comes up with another initiative to enhance this community that's so dedicated to good business and raising healthy families.

The DuPage River, with many natural attributes, created a great place to build a successful community.

We strive to do our very best every day, mainly because our community — our people — wouldn't want it any other way.

A. George Pradel, 40th Mayor of Naperville

Foreword by Mayor A. George Pradel 5

Yesterday and Today..8

Close to Home 26

At Home in the Heartland 56

A Lifetime of Learning 80

Making an Impact...104

It's Our Business 128

Advertisers Index 150

Good Sources

    About Naperville for All of Us! 152

Photo by Jefferey Ross

John Deere Highlander Plow (1897)
Purchased from Lewis A. Reiche,
at the corner of Main & Jackson
by Adam Meisinger (owner of the plow).
Donated by Earl Meisinger Family.

YESTERDAY AND

Our community is as rich in culture and

history as it is in beautiful scenery, fun

places and great people.

aperville's can-do spirit pioneer spirit of adventure, enriched with dedication to its heritage, keeps residents moving forward and moving here.

Thanks to local visionaries who saved structure after structure from the wrecking ball during Naperville's growth age of the 1960s and 1970s, Naper Settlement is a repository for many buildings and artifacts where you can "visit yesterday today."

No two people see history in the same light. Depending upon where you sit, who you know, what newspapers you read or television you watch, your recollection of the past and recent events is based on your personal experiences and interpretation.

Some folks are great storytellers, able to embellish an event few people will recognize. Other witnesses stick to the facts, but omit some of them. Even the eye of a camera can focus on history in ways that send many different messages.

The reflections in this volume, a showcase of Naperville at 175 years, only begin to tell the story about this fascinating city.

In addition to Naper Settlement, thousands of commemorative bricks, plaques and medallions recognize generous contributors along the Naperville Riverwalk. The Century Walk outdoor art exhibit recounts lessons learned about earning a living, giving back to the community and making a difference.

The shelves at the Naperville Public Library and local bookshops are filled with volumes about local history.

And Naperville Community Television-Channel 17, local public access TV, cablecasts documentaries, ribbon cuttings and featured programs produced by member producers.

To celebrate the 175th anniversary of the founding of Naperville, Co-Chairs Mayor George Pradel and Councilwoman Mary Ellingson and their Central Committee created a theme: "Heritage, Unity and Vision."

To commemorate this historic anniversary — 75 years after Centennial Beach and 25 years after the Riverwalk began — residents of all ages, service organizations and businesses were encouraged to plan events for calendar dates of their choice.

In addition, three dates were selected for citywide celebrations well in advance to enhance the themes: New Year's Day "Heritage," January 1, 2006; Naper Days "Unity," June 17, 2006, and Frontier Park "Vision," October 14, 2006.

Eager to **embrace change** and

challenges, Naperville continues

to develop into a beautiful,

booming community with

neighborly, caring citizens.

From lampposts to subdivisions

and from **historic** downtown to

new planned living centers,

citizens **share a mission** to

maintain the city's most

cherished **family values**.

Joe Naper

Born 1798 in Shaftsbury, Vermont

Died August 1862 in Naperville

Great Lakes Sea Captain.

Pioneer. Visionary. **Founder of Naperville.**

Surveyor. Husband to Almeda.

Father of six. Grandfather of seven.

Lumber Miller. Mason. Philanthropist.

School Superintendent. Soldier.

First President of the Village Board.

State Legislator.

Pictured here in 1886 as the Naperville Light Guard, with roots back to 1859, the Naperville Municipal Band is one of America's oldest community bands. With nearly 100 active members today, the band performs throughout the year with a 10-week series of outdoor summer concerts at the Naperville Community Concert Center in Central Park and three indoor seasonal concerts in local auditoriums.

Photo courtesy of Naperville Heritage Society

Photo courtesy of Naperville Heritage Society

Les Schrader

Local artist and sign painter Les Schrader, born in 1907, spent almost half of the 20th century interpreting Naperville's 19th-century history in his paintings. Today, 42 of his paintings, depicting such scenes as the arrival of Joe Naper and families in a Conestoga Wagon and the development of the city through Victorian times, are on display in "Brushstrokes of the Past." This permanent exhibit, located in the lower-level history gallery of the Pre-Emption House, is a popular stop in the gateway to Naper Settlement.

Hannah Ditzler Alspaugh

Certainly unaware of her future impact, Hannah Ditzler Alspaugh could be considered Naperville's first journalist for the schools. She kept diaries about her life and the Naper Academy from 1848 to 1873. Her detailed accounts of the early educational opportunities in Naperville are now preserved in the archival library at Naper Settlement. Visitors can schedule access to her collective works as well as to several hundred volumes pertaining to history of Naperville, DuPage County, and the State of Illinois.

Photo courtesy of Naperville Heritage Society

Bailey Hobson

Bailey Hobson, a miller, tavern keeper, farmer and political leader, was also recognized as the first white settler in what is now DuPage County. Hobson's grist mill was just down the DuPage River, about a mile from Joe Naper's saw mill. Today, in Pioneer Park, the original grist stones have been preserved as a monument to one of Naperville's earliest families.

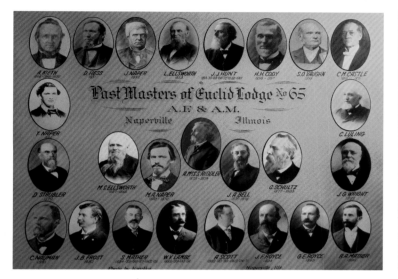

Captain Joe Naper's example of service, charity and dedication to the community has been passed down through the generations. Many of today's leaders credit his pioneer spirit for the success of this dynamic city, with so many thriving service clubs and volunteer organizations.

Naper's affiliation with Naperville's oldest social and fraternal organization — Euclid Lodge of Ancient Free and Accepted Masons, which was founded on September 28, 1848 — provides another glimpse of Naperville's namesake.

According to a history compiled by Robert Stockner, a gathering of Naperville men — Joseph Naper, Aylmer Keith, Nathan Allen, Lewis Ellsworth and others who perhaps had tired of traveling to meetings in St. Charles — petitioned the Grand Lodge of Illinois to form a Naperville Lodge of Masons. The Grand Master of the Most Honorable Society of Free and Accepted Masons of Illinois subsequently granted Euclid Lodge No. 65 its constitution on October 2, 1849.

Upon receiving its charter, Euclid first met in a room on the upper floor of the DuPage Cash Store. In 1852, when Joseph Naper was Worshipful Master, the Lodge moved to the third story of Union Hall, later known as the Martin Becker Building.

The Lodge remained in the Union Hall until 1857, when a major flood of the DuPage River wiped out the Washington Street Bridge and damaged properties in downtown Naperville.

As an aside, also in 1857, the first Village Board of Trustees was elected, with Naper as the first president. In addition, neighbors up north who wanted a more central location for county government began to challenge Naperville's recognition as the DuPage County Seat.

Embracing Naper's interest to support education, the Lodge donated $150 to Naper Academy, which had opened in 1852 at the west end of Van Buren Avenue, where Naper School is today. As a result, a special room on the north side of the second floor was constructed especially for the Lodge, where members met regularly until Naper's death in 1862. Records note that Masonic burial services for "Worshipful Brother Naper" were held in the Naperville Cemetery on August 24,1862, "with usual Masonic simplicity."

In 1934, Delmar Kroehler presented the Euclid Lodge with the "Oriental Chair," artistically hand-carved in his furniture factory, now the landmark known as Fifth Avenue Station on the north side of the Burlington tracks. Today the handsome chair sits prominently in the Euclid Lodge, where the Ancient Free and Accepted Masons continue to meet in their present location at 34 West Jefferson Avenue.

Cigar making was a thriving business for the operators of the William Knoch factory, pictured in the store in the 1920s. The William Knoch cigar store and factory stood on the southeast corner of Jefferson Avenue at Main Street. According to accounts in Genevieve Towsley's *Historic Naperville*, cigar making was discontinued here in 1933. Of course, today, the community sports many cigar-smoking gentlemen and women.

Heim's Confectionery, operated by Julian Heim, thrived for a time on West Jefferson Avenue near Main Street in the early 1900s. The standard confectionery and cigar store was a precursor to today's sweet shops with soft ice cream, bakeries with soup and sandwiches, coffee shops with coffee cakes, and Internet cafés with access to the world.

Naperville has always been a place of adventure where you could enjoy the surroundings.
More and more, folks are looking for alternatives to driving automobiles!

Some things haven't changed through the ages. From triathlons to Rotary Ride, bicyclists gear up to compete in annual events.

The people of Naperville care about their **families** and their **roots**. The LDS Family History Center is **dedicated** to helping those who **seek** for clues that may give them a glimpse into their **ancestry** and **heritage**.

The West Branch of the DuPage River attracted Naperville's earliest settlers, commanding a major role in the city's commerce, success and recreation.

All sorts of educational and cultural activities have appeal at Naper Settlement, a 19th-century living history museum. Established in 1969 when St. John's Episcopal Church, now known as Century Memorial Chapel, was saved from demolition and moved to the grounds of the Martin Mitchell Mansion, the accredited museum has developed into an outdoor village, thriving in a beautifully landscaped 13-acre setting.

In the lower level of the Pre-Emption House, the gateway to Naper Settlement, an exhibit titled "Brushstrokes of the Past" pays tribute to local artist Les Schrader, instilling an appreciation for Naperville's development from a pioneer outpost in 1831 to a bustling turn-of-the-century community. Patrons connect with the past as Schrader's 42 paintings tell the story of Naperville. Naper Settlement curators have enhanced the permanent exhibit with other artifacts, photos and memorabilia, reflecting the vast contrasts in lifestyles throughout the 19th century until now.

ST. JOHN'S EPISCOPAL CHURCH

St. John's Episcopal Church
750 W. Aurora Ave.
Naperville, IL 60540
630.355.0467
stjohns-episcopal.com

In 1838, a Joliet missionary conducted the first Episcopal services in Naperville area. The Parish of St. John's Episcopal Church was officially organized on June 4, 1850.

In 1863 a parishioner donated land for construction of a meeting place, and a striking American Gothic-style building was started in 1864. The building opened for worship on January 1, 1865. Rapid growth of the parish occurred during the 1870s, and the congregation quickly outgrew its building. Workmen cut the building in half, moved the sanctuary back, and added transepts and a chancel, producing the building's final cruciform shape.

Following the end of the second World War, Naperville entered a time of growth — and so did St. John's. By the mid-1960s, the congregation had once again outgrown its home. The parish voted to construct a new church. The original building was donated to the newly formed Naperville Heritage Society and moved to what is now known as Naper Settlement. The new church was dedicated in September 1972, and growth of the parish continued. An addition was constructed in 1990, and a major renovation and enlargement of the facilities was completed in 2002.

Today the congregation of St. John's serves and supports not only each other, but also the entire community. No matter what your denomination or background, St. John's welcomes you with open arms to explore our parish. St. John's spiritual development and community outreach programs offer parishioners the opportunity to strengthen their faith while serving. Among the many programs are:
* Brotherhood of St. Andrew
* Daughters of the King
* Men's Group
* Precepts Bible Study
* Sing and Play
* Women's Ministries
* Habitat for Humanity
* St. John's Pennywise Shoppe, a resale outlet to raise money for community outreach
* Christian-based Preschool
* Cathedral Shelter Christmas Baskets
* St. Hilarious

Welcome to St. John's Episcopal Church and our faith community. We hope you will join us in seeking to be faithful disciples of our Lord.

[top] Old St. John's Episcopal Church, constructed in 1864, is now part of Naperville Heritage Society's Naper Settlement. [bottom] The current St. John's Episcopal Church building was dedicated in 1972 and renovated and enlarged in 2002.

**Naperville Area
Chamber of Commerce**
55 South Main Street
Suite 351
Naperville, IL 60540
630.355.4141
www.naperville.net

The Naperville Area Chamber of Commerce was originally founded in 1913 as the Naperville Association of Commerce. Today, we are a business organization comprised of more than 2,000 companies of all sizes who take advantage of the opportunities for marketing, networking and professional development that we provide. We also act as "the Business Voice," communicating the positions of business people on important legislative issues to local, state and federal lawmakers.

Eighteen full-time employees and an equivalent number of part-time employees and interns are hard at work every business day to provide the best services and support for our 2,000 Member businesses. Additionally, we field thousands of inquiries from prospective new residents and businesses each year, directing new clients to the great services our Members provide.

Through the commitment and involvement of our Members, the Naperville Area Chamber of Commerce provides leadership for the benefit of the business community by promoting economic opportunities, advocating the interests of business, providing Members with education and resources, and encouraging mutual support.

A HISTORY OF SERVICE

The Chamber's many accomplishments over the years include:

- Working to improve the city's streets and sidewalks as far back as 1917
- Helping with the formation of the Naperville Park District in 1966
- Instituting the Community Leadership Program in 1983
- Establishing our website in 1995
- Founding the Small Business of the Year Awards program in 1998
- Helping form the Downtown Naperville Alliance of downtown businesses and property owners in 2001
- Opening a branch office in south Naperville in 2002
- Moving to a new headquarters and adopting a new identity and focus in 2004

The Chamber's rich history has built a foundation for the organization as we enter a new era approaching the end of our first century in business.

WE'RE PROUD OF OUR CHAMBER, OUR MEMBERS AND OUR COMMUNITY

Without the support of the Naperville community and our Members, all of the work and accomplishments of the Naperville Area Chamber of Commerce would not have been possible. We are proud to congratulate the City of Naperville for 175 glorious years. There's no place in the world that we'd rather be a part of, and we're proud to contribute to Naperville's ongoing success.

"My business has grown because our community is aware of the importance of partnerships between business and all entities involved in making Naperville a great place to live."

- Mary Ann Bobosky, Advocates Building Communities, Inc.

"Business has been the engine that has driven the phenomenal growth of our community. We are all very proud of 175 years of community progress and success."

- Mike Skarr, President & CEO, NACC

"I love doing business in Naperville! I have been in business in other great towns, but none can match the spirit of the community and the dedication of the key people that make things happen in this great city. We, as a company, have been blessed by the opportunity to do business here."

- Dan Casey, Casey's Foods

"When I became aware of the impact that my community and my Chamber had on the initial growth of my business as well as the current growth, I realized the value in being involved in the community and being a Chamber member."
– Nicki Anderson, Reality Fitness

"Naperville is a great place to do business because of the spirit of cooperation that exists between the businesses, the community, local governments and the schools. Whether it is civic causes, quality of life, business development, or our kids' education, you can count on the stakeholders in Naperville pulling together to make this a better place to live, raise a family and do business."
– Brad McGuire, Jackson Moving & Storage

"This community of Naperville has allowed us to make our livelihood since 1975. It is for that reason that we do what we can to give back to the community. I believe that quality attracts quality. If we all work to make Naperville a quality place to live and raise your family, then we will attract quality people who will continue that tradition."
- John Schmitt, john greene Realtor

"Businesses contribute greatly to the economic viability of a community by employing people who buy goods and services, volunteer in our schools, and genuinely care about the quality of life they are able to achieve. Being involved in your community is a responsibility you must take seriously if you are to be successful. The opportunity to impact your community through your actions is the true measure of a person. The Naperville community has a rich history of entrepreneurs who have helped shape our past and no doubt will guide us in the future."
– Ray Kinney, MinuteMan Press

"It's the commitment of a community like Naperville that should be duplicated throughout this wonderful country; it opens it arms to every immigrant that is willing to participate in collaboration for a better community and a better world. GRACIAS TO ALL!"

May your God take you by his hand and never let you go.

Remain humble that is the essence of remaining human.
- Roberto Ramirez, Tidy International

"MidAmerica Bank has been in the Naperville Community since 1974 and we have seen a tremendous amount of growth during that time. With our business emphasis on Mortgage Loans, we have helped countless Napervillians realize their dream of home ownership in this wonderful town. Thanks to Naperville and its management, our business continues to grow."
- Loretta Karkhoff, MidAmerica Bank

Seize the future. Grasp tomorrow's opportunity today. Watch for it. Recognize its potential. Seize it.

"A vibrant business community has always been vital to the health of Naperville. Businesses provide the goods and services that make the quality of our lives so high. Taxes from businesses support the school systems that are essential to our community. Businesses also provide jobs, which are the lifeblood of a strong city. The Naperville Area Chamber of Commerce has played, and continues to play, a major role in ensuring that our business community remains healthy for the benefit of all Naperville residents."
-Steve Frost, Pedersen & Houpt

"Naperville and the Chamber have been the most significant factors influencing the growth of my business and my personal development. The networking available at our meetings and committees is fantastic, while the high-quality seminars and speakers have motivated me to expand my horizons."
– Art Littlefield, Financial Strategies & Solutions Group

"SBC Illinois has always worked hard to develop and maintain strong relationships with the communities the company serves. We are proud to be a Member of the Chamber. It provides a forum to exchange ideas as well as to keep open an important line of communication between the company and local businesses and consumers."
– Valerie Bruggeman, SBC Illinois

"As president of FASTSIGNS, I can say the basis of our past success has been in direct proportion to the level of our active participation in the community and the Chamber."
– Shane Beard, FASTSIGNS

"Harris N.A. is proud to be a part of a dynamic growth oriented business community. It has truly been a win-win experience."
- David M. Wrobel, Harris N.A.

"We have had tremendous success in Naperville and if I had to attribute it to one thing it would be our understanding of the needs of the families and businesses who choose Naperville as their home. Our understanding has been developed through 25 years of experience in serving our clients and in the wonderful training provided by the many Chamber-sponsored seminars, management series and colorful speakers and writers. Our clients expect prompt and excellent service at a reasonable fee... and that is what we strive to deliver to each and every client...whether the matter be great or small."
– Dick Kuhn, Kuhn, Heap & Monson, Attorneys at Law

"Giving back to the community has meant so much to our company and has brought greater recognition of our business in the greater Naperville area."
– Roger Hart, CBIZ

"Success is a journey of a continuous investment in your team, your guests and your community"
- Hossein Jamali, Meson Sabika

CLOSE TO

Working together, local governments, independent businesses and private citizens have created a rich culture — a diverse culture Naperville citizens continually try to define.

Naperville's heritage spans three centuries. Our pioneer spirit of adventure continues to travel unmarked paths to a better future, as citizens embrace public/private partnerships for many of the solutions to the challenges that unite them.

Since Naperville celebrated its sesquicentennial in 1981, the Riverwalk has grown to nearly four miles of winding paths from Jefferson Avenue to Hillside Road, with a magnificent gateway to downtown known as Fredenhagen Park.

Century Walk, an outdoor public art project with plans for 30 pieces, has grown to include 24 works of art, reflecting memorable people, places and events from the 20th century.

The Moser Tower, with a 72-bell carillon — one of the four largest in the world — was built at the foot of Rotary Hill to commemorate the new millennium.

Naper Settlement, a 13-acre, 19th-century living history outdoor museum, received accreditation in 2002 by the American Association of Museums. Of some 8,500 museums across the nation, only about 770 are accredited, and Naper Settlement is the only outdoor museum accredited in Illinois.

The DuPage Children's Museum opened in 2001 at the site of the old Moser Lumber Yard.

The nationally recognized Naperville Public Library has grown to include three state-of-the-art facilities, the newest at 95th Street.

The Community First, a grassroots initiative, has enlightened local residents, builders and architects on how to work together to address the important and emotional issue of redevelopment in established neighborhoods.

And the Naperville Community Concert Center enhances Central Park with a permanent facility for the Naperville Municipal Band and other performing arts groups.

Pfeiffer Hall and other venues on the campus of North Central College offer opportunities from intimate theater to Broadway-type musicals and string ensembles to jazz bands. The performing arts are celebrated, with big plans to expand venues waiting in the wings.

During 2006, North Central expects to break ground on a fine arts center that could play a role in creating a theater district in the heart of downtown. The state-of-the-art facility is planned for the corner of Chicago Avenue at Ellsworth, a cultural center Naperville's college and arts communities richly deserve.

Naperville celebrates annual festivals and parades, organized by service organizations and volunteers, with a vitality that connects its citizens with patriotism, pride and achievement.

The Kiwanis Pancake Festival, St. Patrick's Day Parade, Memorial Day Parade, Exchange Club's Ribfest, Jaycees Last Fling, Naperville Art League Riverwalk Fine Art Fair, Rotary Oktoberfest and the Grand Illumination are among dozens of annual special events that capture the compassion for humanity and strong sense of community that began here in 1831.

The Spirit of the American Doughboy, a sculpture to honor World War I infantrymen, sits in Burlington Square Park to welcome visitors as they arrive at the communter train stop.

Picturesque galleries and noteworthy bookshops provide ample places to browse in downtown Naperville while waiting for a table at many fine and casual dining establishments.

Windows display all the offerings of seasonal flings and tempting things.

Since 1981, the Naperville Riverwalk has captured the fancy of the community.

Begun with local dollars and cooperative volunteer spirit in celebration of the city's 150th birthday, the Riverwalk today features nearly four miles of walking paths. The main path, built of signature serpentine bricks, follows the bend of the West Branch of the DuPage River, creating a natural southern border for Naperville's central business district, where plenty of restaurants and shopping suit every taste.

First conceived as a rebuilding of the Centennial Beach walkway along the river, the vision for the Riverwalk has developed into the community's "crown jewel," with fountains, sculptures, covered bridges, gazebos and playgrounds. The Riverwalk Eatery and the Grand Pavilion provide places for picnics and reunions near Centennial Beach.

In recent years, the park has been enhanced with commemoratives such as Rotary Hill for sledding, the Jaycees Marina with paddleboats, an amphitheater with the Celebration 2000 Millennium Wall and Labyrinth, and the Moser Tower with the Millennium Carillon.

A memorial to all victims of the September 11, 2001, attack on America is located on the Riverwalk's south bank, adjacent to the Naperville Municipal Center.

A little farther east, near the Washington Street Bridge, Fredenhagen Park welcomes walkers for peaceful reflection around the Exchange Club Memories Fountain.

Open year-round, the nationally recognized, award-winning linear park is one of the most beautiful gathering places in the Midwest, creating a perfect setting for special events throughout the year from Jefferson Avenue to Hillside Road.

Along with many other annual events such as the **Jaycees Last Fling**, Exchange Club Ribfest and **Rotary Clubs' Oktoberbest**, Naper Days brings **families together** for fun and festivities. Every year, more than **1 million charitable dollars** go back into the community, thanks to the fundraising success of these events.

What's more, the **Downtown Naperville Alliance** puts on a few special events, too. When the sixth book by J.K. Rowling, *Harry Potter and the Half-Blood Prince*, became available, merchants staged a **spectacular event**, transforming the streets of downtown Naperville into **Muggle Magic** for all ages.

Photo by The Naperville Development Partnership and Visitor's Bureau

Private and public facilities focused on good health and recreation provide plenty of opportunities to stay in shape. Residents of all ages are encouraged to dive right into activities that include cooking lessons, team sports, dancing and dozens more to keep healthy hearts, reduce stress and produce great mental attitudes.

The health benefits of regular exercise are endless. Even casual walking on a regular basis bolsters good physical benefits. That's probably why the Riverwalk and other walking paths — such as those in the Springbrook Prairie Forest Preserve — are popular destinations 365 days a year.

Since 1926, hundreds of well-known performing artists have graced the stage of Pfeiffer Hall. Vibrant theater programs by North Central, the Naperville-North Central College Performing Arts Association and the DuPage Symphony Orchestra, as well as a variety of guest lecturers, fill the performance venue throughout the year.

Live performances at North Central College will be enhanced when a 300-seat theater is completed in the former Evangelical Church at 31 S. Ellsworth Street.

Opposite Page The Fredenhagen Park Clock Tower is the new landmark in the place where Prince Castles and later Cock Robin Ice Cream Restaurants reigned from 1931–2000. Today the popular gathering place is a gateway park in tribute to Grace and Walter Fredenhagen, complete with a fitting Century Walk sculpture depicting a likeness of the generous couple titled "Two in a Million," a play on the tag line for the famous "One in a Million" milkshakes.

Located at the base of Rotary Hill along the Riverwalk, the magnificent Millennium Carillon in the Moser Tower was introduced during a spectacular Independence Day concert on June 29, 2000. Amid the roar of cannons and the musical accompaniment of the Naperville Municipal Band and the Naperville Men's Glee Club and Festival Chorus, an estimated 15,000 people in attendance applauded the historic event.

With 72 bronze bells ranging in weight from 10 pounds to the 6-ton "Captain Joseph Naper Bell," the Moser Tower is home to one of the four largest carillons in the world. Musical selections are played at set times daily on about half the bells by a computerized system of strikers.

The largest bell, nicknamed "Big Joe," has a 600-pound clapper and is inscribed, "Celebrating the Spirit of Naperville."

In the tradition of Centennial Beach and the Riverwalk, the Millennium Carillon is a gift from the people of the Naperville community for all future generations to enjoy. The 158-foot-tall tower is named for benefactors Margaret and Harold Moser.

Naperville's most prominent figure on the musical scene exists today because of the generous gifts of time and financial resources and the dedication of thousands of Napervillians who helped with Phase 1. Future plans for Phase 2 include an elevator and a stairway in the Moser Tower, open to an upper-level observation deck accessible to visitors.

Of the 600 carillons worldwide — some of which date back to 15th-century Europe — the Millennium Carillon is one of only four spanning a full six octaves. It is properly known as a Grand Carillon.

Each of the 72 bells, cast at the Royal Eijsbouts Bell Foundry in the Netherlands, is tuned in chromatic scale, much like the strings of a piano. The musical instrument is played by a carillonneur who strikes a mechanical oak keyboard called a clavier, located 100 feet high up in the glass cabin between the two massive bell chambers.

Photo by Jeffery Ross

Photo by Jeffery Ross

Periodically throughout the day, the 72 bells of the Millennium Carillon ring out along the Riverwalk. The melodious sound echoes throughout the community, a timely reminder of a vibrant past where dedicated people have worked together to achieve big things for Naperville.

Whether architecture, culinary arts, theater, music, dance or visual arts, Naperville's appreciation for the finer things in life is always growing in diversity. More and more, the community provides creative outlets for citizens to express themselves and fulfill their individual talents. Many hands-on experiences at art studios and museums can ignite a youngster's passion for history and culture.

Naperville's diversity is captured in more than 70 places of worship.

BBM INCORPORATED

Dwight Yackley is founder of BBM Incorporated, a Naperville-based real estate development and management firm that has its future as well as its roots planted firmly in the city of Naperville.

BBM is building the future while honoring the past. The integrity of each project captures the quality and soul of the community and defines BBM's uniqueness. The quality of design, construction and tenants are hallmarks of BBM. Individually, Yackley secures this legacy by continuing to raise the bar on every development. This commitment is evident in the 1998 landmark building, "Washington Corners," which features anchor tenant Barnes & Noble Bookstore, and the new "Main Street Promenade," which opened in 2004. These developments offer forward-thinking uses with an eye to the past in design. BBM is proud to offer Naperville the best of fine dining, vibrant shopping and class A office space. BBM invests more to make sure each project enhances the community not just for the present, but also well into the future.

Dwight Yackley and BBM have been involved in this community in a fundamental way for more than 20 years.

Yackley is most proud of BBM's dedication to maintaining Naperville's small-town charm and important history. His personal commitment to each project demonstrates his dedication to Naperville in every phase of his work.

BBM Inc.
236 S. Washington
Naperville, IL 60540
630.305.7171
www.bbmincorporated.com

Dwight Yackley, founder of BBM Incorporated, makes sure that all the company's developments — like Washington Corners, anchored by Barnes & Noble Bookstore — blend form and function to truly capture the historic spirit of the community.

Naperville Township
139 Water Street
Naperville, IL 60540-5384
630.355.2786
(fax) 630.637.8380
www.NapervilleTownship.com

Elected Officials
2005-2009

George D. Porter
Supervisor/Treasurer

Gary J. Vician
Trustee

Fred A. Spitzzeri
Trustee

Esin G. Busche
Trustee

May Yurgaitis
Trustee

Carol L. Bertulis
Clerk

Warren L. Dixon, Jr.
Assessor

Stan Wojtasiak
Highway
Commissioner

Township government is one of the oldest forms of government in the United States, predating even the United States Constitution. Most township lines are drawn in a square, six miles on each side. When the country's population lived in mostly rural areas, this guaranteed that no one was more than six miles from local government. Today Illinois still has over 1,400 townships. The City of Naperville lies in portions of six townships.

The most visible of these is Naperville Township, located along the Riverwalk in the downtown area. Eight officials, including the trustees, supervisor, highway commissioner, assessor and township clerk, are elected every four years. They meet publicly twice each month. The second Tuesday in April, all townships in the state have an "old fashioned town meeting," reminiscent of pioneering days.

NAPERVILLE TOWNSHIP OFFICIALS

The role of Naperville Township, like other townships, is unique. The township's elected officials each perform important specific roles:

- All the commercial and residential assessments within the township's borders are conducted by the assessor's office. The assessor's office also assists residents with real estate tax exemptions.
- The highway commissioner, as the elected official in charge of the township road district, is responsible for maintaining all streets and roads in unincorporated areas and working cooperatively with other units of local government to guarantee efficiency.

In 1995, Naperville Township decided to raze the existing administrative building, located on Naperville's Riverwalk, to make room for a new structure that would maximize the valuable site. The new 7,500-square-foot facility, designed by Oppermann Bilsland Architects of Naperville, is the focus of the governmental campus and provides a welcoming entry to the Riverwalk. Hand-moulded brick with stone accents articulates the enduring qualities and civic character of the oldest form of government in the country. Rimmed with windows and capped with an exposed wood structure, the clock tower is a feature both on the interior and exterior. The building also offers scenic views of the Riverwalk.

- The town clerk is the "keeper" of the official seal and maintains public records according to law. The clerk also coordinates voter registration and U.S. Passport services at the township office.
- The four trustees and the supervisor are the voting members of the town board. The trustees are responsible for approving the budgets and ensuring expenditures stay within budget during the year.
- The supervisor is referred to in the state statutes as the "C.E.O." of the township and is treasurer of all town and road district funds, as well as administrator of general and emergency assistance programs plus other "special services."

EMERGENCY ASSISTANCE

If people are not eligible for public aid or unemployment compensation, they are automatically considered for general or emergency assistance programs in times of need. When facing life-threatening situations, such as evictions, heat shutoff and so on, people can turn to the township to help them. Applications can be made quickly and effectively.

SENIOR CITIZENS PROGRAMS

Naperville Township has an extremely active program for senior citizens. Working in cooperation with local law enforcement departments, the township offers TRIAD, a program to educate older citizens about crimes that affect them. Naperville Township also supports transportation for the elderly, Senior Home Sharing and Ecumenical Adult Day Care.

ASSISTANCE FOR FAMILIES

Required to have a program for troubled youth and families, Naperville Township provides funds to NCO Youth & Family Services to support counseling and emergency food and shelter for young people. Naperville Township also supports holiday food basket and adopt-a-family programs, as well as low-income legal assistance for qualified residents and many other special services.

The Naperville Township Road District, led by the highway commissioner, is responsible for maintaining all streets and roads in unincorporated areas.

Atwell-Hicks
www.atwell-hicks.com

NAPERVILLE AND ATWELL-HICKS
SHARING MILESTONES — SHARING GROWTH

Atwell-Hicks Regional Vice President Steven A. D'Anna looks forward to the company's long and prosperous future in Naperville.

This is a big year for Naperville and Atwell-Hicks, the national development consulting firm. Both are celebrating milestone years — 175 for Naperville, and 100 for Atwell-Hicks.

"We are proud to be a new part of Naperville's history," said Atwell-Hicks Regional Vice President Steven A. D'Anna. "As we look over the last 100 years of our company's achievements, we look to Naperville to be a valuable part of our future."

Atwell-Hicks opened its Naperville office in 2001. It is an award-winning, 350-person, development consulting firm focusing on five key service areas: civil engineering, land surveying, land planning, environmental consulting, and water and wastewater design/build services. The company specializes in serving the private land development market.

> *This is a key market for our company. We have already had four years of great success. Our engineers, surveyors and development consultants are here to help shape the foundation for the future. We're here to stay.*

Recently, the firm received national recognition for being named the no. 2 Civil Engineering Firm to Work for by *CE News Magazine*, an industry trade publication that ranks firms with best practices annually. Atwell-Hicks was also recognized by the National Society of Professional Engineers (NSPE) with their annual Private Practice Development Award, which recognized the firm's internal training program, Atwell-Hicks University.

Atwell-Hicks continues to expand operations and services, which also increased their positioning on the *Engineering News-Record* Top 500 Design Firm lists, ranking in the top 200 for the first time in 2005 at 195. The firm entered the list in 1999 at 485 and is one of only five firms to have achieved such a positive increase during that time.

In February, as part of the firm's 100th birthday, all employees and a guest were invited aboard the *Sovereign of the Seas* for a four-day Caribbean cruise to celebrate the company's centennial milestone and enjoy an extended weekend filled with rest, relaxation and lots of fun.

Naperville and Atwell-Hicks have more in common than just celebrating significant anniversary years.

"Naperville is enjoying a tremendous growth. The community retains its traditions but is moving forward with new opportunities for its residents and businesses," said D'Anna.

As Naperville grows, so grows Atwell-Hicks — in 2004 the company reported $44 million in revenues, a record breaking 53 percent growth rate over the previous

> *Naperville is enjoying a tremendous growth. The community retains its traditions but is moving forward with new opportunities for its residents and businesses.*

year. The company also has aggressive plans to expand operations throughout Chicagoland and nationally.

D'Anna joined Atwell-Hicks' Naperville office after relocating from Buffalo, New York, where he was active in local politics and community initiatives. D'Anna believes strongly in community participation where you live and work, by supporting local initiatives and improvement efforts.

This philosophy has followed D'Anna to Naperville, where he has planted himself in the local terra firma by becoming active in the Naperville Chamber of Commerce Young Professionals Network and Naperville Development Partnership. His efforts are supported by the company, which has an excellent reputation for volunteering, with many of the Naperville staff members supporting local charity initiatives, hosting food drives and participating in fundraising events.

D'Anna emphasizes the role his office plays in the firm's overall strategic business plan. "This is a key market for our company. With four years of great success so far, we see Chicagoland as a high-growth market for local land developers, and another location to support our regional and national clients with operations in multiple states."

one word...
PASSION

"Passion" is a key word in the mission of Atwell-Hicks, whose award-winning service has been growing the business at a record rate.

**Naperville
Park District**
320 W. Jackson Ave.
Naperville, IL 60540
630.848.5000
navervilleparks.org

*The Naperville
Park District
has received the
National Park
and Recreation
Association's Gold
Medal Award for
Excellence in Park
and Recreation
Management.*

2006 Milestones
• *Park District's
40th Anniversary*
• *Riverwalk's
25th Anniversary*
• *Centennial Beach's
75th Anniversary*
• *Naperbrook
Golf Course's
15th Anniversary*

**Centennial Beach is a
beloved and historic
part of Naperville.**

In 1964, the Park District Study Committee explored the benefits of establishing a park district for the City of Naperville. At that time, the city owned the municipal park system, which consisted of 218 acres. Foreseeing rapid population growth in the future, the committee determined that the city's current method of acquiring park property solely through donation would not be sufficient for the city's future recreation needs.

The Naperville Park District was created in 1966 and began operations in 1968. The District offered 31 programs in its initial year of operations. Today, the Naperville Park District maintains and operates approximately 2,460 acres comprised of 130 parks; two golf courses; four sports complexes; two inline skating/skateboarding facilities; Centennial Beach; and a multitude of sports fields and courts. The District serves nearly 80,000 participants each year through over 1,000 recreational, arts and environmental programs and events. There are active and passive recreation opportunities for people of all ages and abilities.

Two of the Naperville Park District's facilities present a unique insight into the city's historic commitment to health, recreation and open space.

In 1931, 32 Naperville families contributed $500 each to purchase 45 acres in downtown Naperville for the creation of a park to commemorate Naperville's centennial. The project, constructed by the Work Projects Adminstration, included an aquatic facility: Centennial Beach, which was dedicated on June 6, 1931. The Beach quickly became a prime source of revenue for the city, bringing in $6,000 in its first year alone. Funds from the Beach were used to finance various town projects. In 1955, the Beach hosted Aquathon I, a show

Community commitment and partnerships brought about Naperville's crown jewel, the beautiful Riverwalk.

that included water skiing, diving, high-wire daredevils and synchronized swimmers. By 1969, when the Naperville Park District assumed responsibility for Centennial Beach, years of use had led to marked deterioration. Through the efforts of the Save the Beach Committee, the Beach underwent a series of restorations. In 1981, Centennial Beach celebrated its 50th anniversary with a re-creation of the Aquathons of the 1950s. Between 2002 and 2004, over $2 million in renovations were made to the Beach, including new concrete decks, new circulation systems, new lighting and sound systems, new staircases, and children's play features. Today, Centennial Beach is a beloved and historic part of Naperville.

Community commitment and partnerships also brought about Naperville's crown jewel, the beautiful Riverwalk. A community park that follows the DuPage River through downtown Naperville, Riverwalk was developed in 1981 to commemorate Naperville's sesquicentennial, although it had its origins in a one-mile walkway constructed by the WPA to link Centennial Park with the city's central business district. The Riverwalk was funded exclusively though local dollars, half of which came through donations. It boasts over three miles of beautiful, landscaped brick walking paths and features fountains, covered bridges, an outdoor amphitheater, the Celebration 2000 Wall and Millennium Carillon, gazebos and shaded seating, a cultural center, a large sled hill, the Riverwalk Eatery, a picnic pavilion, and paddleboat rides. The Riverwalk is also surrounded by many fine stores and restaurants.

Unique and beautiful Naperville recreation assets including the Riverwalk, Centennial Beach, two beautiful golf courses, and all of the District's other parks and facilities, would not be possible without the outstanding support the District has received from residents, corporate sponsors, the school districts and volunteers. The Naperville Park District is committed to addressing the needs of a rapidly growing community and has pledged to continue its vital role as a provider of valued programs, services and resources.

Home Improvements USA
480 Industrial Drive
Naperville, IL 60563
630.420.7619

What was once one of Naperville's best-kept secrets isn't a secret anymore — thanks to the enthusiasm of clients all over Chicagoland and across the United States. Home Improvements USA has grown by leaps and bounds since its beginnings in 1993 as Selective Seamless Sidings. In fact, sales of the company's seamless siding, gutter and gutter protection, window, door, and soffit/fascia products more than doubled between 2002 and 2004. This success is no surprise when you review co-owners Steve and Julie Tenute's history of excellence in the home improvement industry.

When he and Julie started their own construction business in 1985, Steve already had several years of experience in the industry. Steve and Julie's commitment to their craft quickly established their reputation as detail-oriented contractors, and they rapidly built a client base among the area's most reputable builders.

In 1990, Steve and Julie switched their focus from new construction to remodeling. In 1993, they purchased a seamless siding machine that had been custom-designed for their own siding. This allowed them to offer a unique and innovative service: seamless siding that was custom-manufactured at the company's own warehouse to fit the exact length of each client's home.

The Tenutes also kept busy developing another product to make life easier for homeowners. Early gutter protection systems often clogged up, creating a nightmare for homeowners. Steve started work on a better solution, tinkering in his garage until he perfected a new invention that he eventually named "Gutter Cap." The Tenutes were granted a patent for the device on October 17, 1995.

Rapid growth soon moved Steve and Julie from their own back yard to a small space on Industrial Drive; further expansion brought a move to two facilities — one at 480 Industrial Drive, which houses manufacturing assembly lines, sales, marketing, administration and corporate offices, and one at 510 Industrial Drive, for warehousing, service, installation and training.

Steve and Julie have always been committed to products of consistently high quality. Gutter Caps are made from a higher-gauge aluminum than that used by competitors, resulting in a stronger finished product. For curb appeal and endurance, Gutter Cap is matched to the color of the client's roof and is treated with a finish that does not fade or chalk. And Steve and Julie have created and patented a special heated version of the Gutter Cap for cold climates. Heater Caps help prevent ice damage to roofs and eliminate icicle formation on gutters.

Home Improvements USA's siding and gutter protection products are custom-manufactured to exactly fit each client's home. Custom color matching and high-quality materials and paint mean the finished result is not only beautiful, but is also guaranteed to last, even in the coldest climates.

Home Improvements USA customer surveys reveal:

"I could mark 'excellent' in every category …but I believe that your company deserves so much more."

"Thank you for being the type of company that we can trust."

"I have already recommended your product to people I know."

In addition to selling and installing seamless siding and gutter caps, the company offers sales and installation of high-quality fascia, windows and doors. Services include a lifetime guarantee on every product installed and a double lifetime guarantee, transferable at no charge to a new homeowner, on the company's own Gutter Cap and Heater Cap. In 2005, the Tenutes renamed their company Home Improvement USA to better represent the diversity of their products and services.

Steve and Julie's goal of selling their products nationwide has also been met. Gutter Cap Inc., a subsidiary of Home Improvement USA, distributes Gutter Cap and Heater Cap to a network of 50 dealers across the United States. Unlike other companies in the gutter protection business, Gutter Cap installers must attend training in Naperville for factory certification.

Outstanding products are delivered with the Tenutes' signature outstanding customer service. Steve and Julie do not want a homeowner's business one time; they want their business for a lifetime. Clients calling Home Improvements USA always reach a real person trained in quality customer service — never a recording. The company has not had one unresolved complaint with the Better Business Bureau since 1993 and has been complaint-free since 2002. And Gutter Cap and Heater Cap have been featured on PBS' "This Old House" and "Ron Hazelton's House Calls" as well as on "Weekend Makeover."

Steve, Julie and their employees give back to the community through events and charities, including the Muscular Dystrophy Association, Loaves and Fishes and Special Olympics. Additionally, with true hometown pride, Steve and Julie look to the Naperville community first when they have hiring needs.

Steve and Julie and the staff of Home Improvements USA congratulate Naperville on reaching a milestone in history and are proud to be a part of this great city.

AnamArt Gallery
103 S. Washington St.
Naperville, IL 60540
630.369.7504
603.369.7508 fax
www.anamartgallery.com
anamartgallery@aol.com

Named for the Gaelic word *anam*, meaning "soul," AnamArt Gallery is a fine art gallery bringing the best in local and national art to Naperville. Owner Joan Hennessy and her staff of ten are proud not only to display original pieces for the enrichment of the community, but also to offer their expertise to art lovers, collectors, designers, businesses and the general public.

Originally located near 87th and Washington in Naperville, in February 2005 AnamArt celebrated its grand opening in a new, spacious, beautifully lighted building in downtown Naperville. The gala event featured a reception for renowned Cincinnati artists, M. Katherine Hurley and M.P. Wiggins, with an exhibit of their colorful, vibrant pieces. Speaking of the event, Hennessy noted with delight the Gallery's new setting in the thriving downtown community and cultural scene. "We are so excited to be here in downtown Naperville," Hennessy said. "Our community is so alive. We hope to add to its charm for residents and tourists by providing only the best in fine art."

Itself a work of art, the new gallery features high ceilings and south and east facing windows, creating a bright, crisp, inviting environment that enhances the viewing experience.

Original 2D and 3D artwork of professional artists working in a variety of media is on display. The collection features both renowned and emerging artists from across the nation. It includes paintings, glass art, ceramics, sculpture and jewelry in styles ranging from traditional to contemporary and even whimsical. The works, in a multitude of styles, colors and price ranges, make AnamArt Gallery a visual feast that will intrigue art lovers.

AnamArt enjoys a prominent role within the growing cultural and educational community in Naperville. The gallery regularly hosts evening Artists' Receptions to help foster a deeper understanding and appreciation of the artists' interpretations. Open to everyone, these receptions offer the opportunity to meet the

In February 2005, AnamArt Gallery celebrated the grand opening of its beautiful new home in downtown Naperville.

talented individuals who create the gallery's works of art. "People may be attracted to the colors or subject matter of a piece, but talking to the artist and understanding his or her inspiration really brings the art to life," said Hennessy.

"Many people are afraid to make a commitment to a piece of art," she added. "We help them trust their own sense of what makes them feel good. Choosing art is not about matching the couch, but is all about adding visual stimulation to your home that makes you smile." The gallery's fine art associates work with clients in their homes and work spaces, bringing a selection of pieces to view in the client's environment. The consultations are complimentary with installation services also available.

As part of its commitment to the community, AnamArt Gallery generously supports the Riverwalk Foundation. The gallery regularly offers Naperville scenic plates with 100% of the proceeds benefiting the Foundation. In 2005, AnamArt sponsored five figures in the Naperville United Way's summer sculpture series. It also hosted a reception for Family Shelter Services to launch their new book, helping to raise funds for the Shelter.

Other special events have focused on particular cultures, styles or media. For example, in March the gallery hosted a St. Pat's Celebration, featuring works by artists of Irish descent. Bagpipe music along with Irish foods and refreshments rounded out the festivities.

Fostering the future of the region's own artists, the AnamArt Gallery sponsored a scholarship competition for college-bound area high school students. Twenty finalists' works of art were displayed at an Artists' Reception honoring the students. The gallery awarded a $1,000 scholarship to the winner. "We are very excited about the quality of the work we received," said Hennessy. "Our vision is to encourage creativity and originality among the students, whether they study art or not."

AnamArt Gallery not only brings residents up close to innovative art and artists, but also helps them to discover their own creative vision. Art workshops that are open to the public allow hands-on exploration of a variety of artistic media.

For more information about AnamArt Gallery's exhibits, special events and hours, visit www.anamartgallery.com or call 630.369.7504.

Vibrant and colorful works of art, from traditional to contemporary to whimsical, grace the walls of the AnamArt Gallery, a fine art gallery bringing the best of both celebrated and evolving artists' work to Naperville.

EDWARD HOSPITAL & HEALTH SERVICES

**Edward Hospital
& Health Services**
801 S. Washington St.
Naperville, IL 60540
630.527.3000
www.edward.org

dward Hospital & Health Services is a full-service, regional health care provider offering access to complex medical specialties and innovative programming for residents of Naperville, Bolingbrook, Lisle, Woodridge, Warrenville, Aurora/Fox Valley, Plainfield, Romeoville and surrounding communities. Edward has earned a reputation as a leader in such areas as imaging technology, care for critically ill newborns, minimally invasive surgery, mind/body wellness classes, advanced cardiac treatments and in vitro fertilization. Edward is also a leader in patient satisfaction.

While Edward has grown tremendously in the past few decades, the genuine concern for patient care stems from its early 20th-century roots. Founded by Eudora Hull Gaylord Spalding in 1907 as a memorial to her husband, Edward Gaylord, the Edward Sanitarium was one of the first treatment centers for tuberculosis in the Great Lakes region. In time, as the epidemic subsided, Edward Sanitarium turned its attention to other, more urgent community needs.

In October 1955, Edward Sanitarium officially reopened its doors as Edward Hospital, an acute care facility with 45 beds. Within the next 10 years, the hospital expanded to 110 beds. As the community continued to grow, Edward Hospital supported its growth by expanding departments, adding patient care units and providing patients with more advanced medical technology.

Over the years Edward Hospital has evolved. Today it's known as Edward Hospital & Health Services. Edward is anchored by Edward Hospital, a full-service, not-for-profit hospital with 236 private rooms, more than 4,000 employees and a medical staff of more than 800 physicians. Edward also includes the Edward Healthcare Centers in Bolingbrook, Naperville and Plainfield; the Edward Heart Hospital; Linden

Oaks Hospital at Edward; the Edward Cancer Center; the Center for Surgery; Edward Medical Group; Edward Women's Center for Health; the Edward Health & Fitness Centers in Naperville and Woodridge; and Charles E. Miller, MD & Associates: Specialists in Reproductive Health at Edward.

In 1991, Edward Hospital completed a $28 million building project that created all-private patient rooms. In 1992, the Edward Hospital Emergency Department was enlarged 2.5 times its previous size, which helped to decrease emergency visit wait times. In 1994, Edward Hospital and Central DuPage Hospital joined

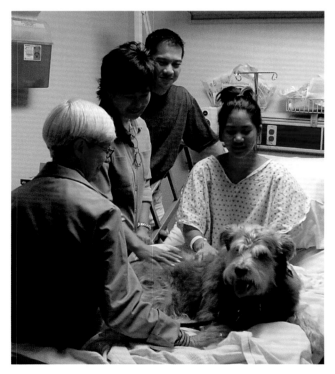

(TOP)
Edward Hospital provides top-notch health care to the entire region.

(BOTTOM RIGHT)
Unique treatments show Edward Hospital's compassion. Studies show that the comfort and happiness brought about by animal visits foster positive patient outcomes.

a group of physicians to open the Center for Surgery in Naperville.

In the mid '90s Edward opened two freestanding health care centers: Edward Healthcare Center/Bolingbrook and Edward Healthcare Center/Naperville. A second fitness center, Edward Health & Fitness Center at Seven Bridges, focusing on family fitness, opened in Woodridge in 1997.

In fall of 1999 Edward purchased Linden Oaks Hospital at Edward, which offers a full spectrum of behavioral health services. Also in 1999, Edward received approval for a $90 million renovation and expansion project to enable the hospital to continue providing high-quality health care to the rapidly growing communities it serves. The project included expanded outpatient services and waiting areas, postpartum beds, an expanded Neonatal Intensive Care Unit, and a new women's imaging suite. Edward also opened new operating rooms equipped with state-of-the-art technology for minimally invasive procedures.

In 2000 and 2001 Edward added a 900-space parking deck and an Education Center. Also in 2000 the hospital opened a Pediatric Emergency Department and achieved a Level III designation for its Neonatal Intensive Care Unit. A Pediatric Intensive Care Unit and a Pediatric Specialties Center were also added in 2001.

The Edward Healthcare Center in Plainfield opened in 2002, offering area residents convenient access to the services of primary care physicians, cardiologists and OB/GYNs.

In the fall of 2002 a 71-bed, all-private-room Heart Hospital opened to provide inpatient cardiac services. This one-stop resource for cardiac care — the first hospital of its kind in Illinois — combines the most advanced technology with every possible patient comfort. The design of the building creates a peaceful ambience. It's a people-friendly environment with extensive use of wood and natural light, rotating local artwork, and even live musicians. A healing garden includes a cascading waterfall, streams and beautiful fish. Behind the looks of a five-star hotel, Edward Heart Hospital is home to innovative cardiac technology. It has advanced cardiac catheterization technology and two state-of-the-art operating rooms to make cardiac surgery more effective. Every member of the Heart Hospital staff focuses exclusively on cardiac care; the cardiologists and cardiac nurses at Edward Heart Hospital are among the nation's most respected. The outpatient cardiac services place a strong focus on preventive medicine and educating patients, with a goal of ultimately eliminating heart disease.

Edward Hospital has also completed a 56,000-square-foot expansion of its Emergency and Pediatric Emergency Departments in 2004. This expansion will allow the hospital to accommodate growth in the volume of Emergency Department visits, while at the same time providing more private and efficient treatment and triage areas for patients.

An expansion project that opened in March 2005, the new Edward Cancer Center is the first in the area to combine leading technology, research, oncologists and clinical staff with unique support services — all in a warm environment that feels like home. A fireplace, floor-to-ceiling windows, soothing live music and amenities that allow family members to stay close by to comfort patients receiving state-of-the-art care that includes the latest cancer-fighting technology and treatments. These include the latest chemotherapy treatments and also intense radiation that conforms to the tumor shape, sparing healthy tissue, and breast cancer therapy that reduces treatment time.

In June 2005, Edward broke ground on the Edward Plainfield Outpatient Center with a scheduled opening of 2006. Services include immediate care, imaging, community education, endoscopy and sleep studies.

Throughout its growth, Edward Hospital has received tremendous support from the community. Because growth has been focused on the special needs of the region it serves, Edward Hospital has truly become a full-service, regional healthcare provider, right in the heart of Naperville.

(LEFT)
Opened in 2004, the aquatic-themed Pediatric Emergency Department provides the best specialized care available for children in a sunny atmosphere that makes the experience less intimidating for kids and parents.

(RIGHT)
Introducing the new Edward Cancer Center—the first in the area to combine leading technology, research and oncologists with unique support services.

The Holiday Inn Select, Naperville's largest hotel, is an award-winning hotel and conference center that plays an important role in the commerce of this community.

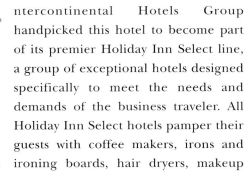

Intercontinental Hotels Group handpicked this hotel to become part of its premier Holiday Inn Select line, a group of exceptional hotels designed specifically to meet the needs and demands of the business traveler. All Holiday Inn Select hotels pamper their guests with coffee makers, irons and ironing boards, hair dryers, makeup mirrors, and well-lit desk work areas. Electronic locks, second phones with dataports, free local calls within 10 miles, on-demand in-room movies, video checkout, voice mail and free high-speed Internet access are additional services that are standard fare at these quality hotels. Further, all registered guests receive a complimentary *USA Today*, delivered to their rooms. The award-winning Holiday Inn Select Naperville has 426 guest rooms, including executive and parlor suites. Many health-conscious guests also utilize the hotel's indoor pool, fitness center and game room.

Numerous dining choices are available at the Holiday Inn Select, from casual breakfast or luncheon buffets to elegant dining in the Grand Ballroom. While talking in a relaxed atmosphere under the Terrace Café's skylit atrium, guests enjoy a delicious variety of meals, fresh salad bars and homemade desserts. The Terrace Bar is another popular spot where business associates meet and unwind after a busy day.

Providing abundant facilities for any large event or conference, the hotel also offers 27,000 square feet of meeting space, including a 6,400-square-foot Grand Ballroom. A full-service audiovisual department furnishes equipment and expertise for a wide range of presentations, while the hotel's sales and catering department provides professional guidance to help businesses and families customize plans and menus for any occasion.

Conveniently located on Naper Boulevard, adjacent to the East-West Tollway/Interstate 88, the Holiday Inn Select is a short drive from many of Naperville's popular attractions, such as Naper Settlement, the Riverwalk and the community's historic downtown. Other popular tourist destinations, such as the Morton Arboretum, Billy Graham Center, Cantigny Gardens and Museum, Oak Brook Shopping Center, Paramount Arts Center, Hollywood Riverboat Casino, and the new Chicago Premium Outlet Mall are also nearby. The hotel's quick accessibility to O'Hare and Midway airports downtown Chicago, and the northwestern suburbs via Interstates 294 and 355 makes it a popular choice of meeting planners and visitors alike.

Holiday Inn Select's 6,400-square-foot Grand Ballroom is available for special occasions.

Its premier location is close to major area businesses, such as BP, Tellabs, Lucent Technologies, Nalco, Laidlaw Transit, Millward Brown, General Motors and ConAgra Foods. Many of these companies make the Holiday Inn Select their first choice when arranging accommodations for their employees, clients and corporate guests. Many choose this hotel and conference center when planning their training seminars, conferences and special events.

The Holiday Inn Select, Naperville's largest hotel,

> *An award-winning hotel and conference center that plays an important role in the commerce of this community.*

is an award-winning hotel and conference center that plays an important role in the commerce of this community. A local landmark, the hotel opened as the first full-service hotel in Naperville in 1981. The facility underwent a major renovation in April 2002.

Since its inception, the Holiday Inn Select Naperville has been recognized for high levels of quality and achievement. After its first year of operation, the hotel won Holiday Inn Worldwide's Newcomer of the Year Award, one of only 14 new Holiday Inns in the world selected for meeting the highest standards of quality and customer service. Then, in 1994, the hotel won the Torchbearer Award, the highest award presented by Holiday Inn Worldwide. Naperville's Holiday Inn Select was one of only 20 hotels in the world to receive this coveted honor. In 1995 and 1996, the hotel also received national Quality Excellence Awards, given only to hotels achieving distinction in all aspects of their operations.

The Holiday Inn Select's excellence is not limited to the customers it serves within its spacious rooms. Its excellence extends into the community as well. Recognizing the value businesses can bring to schools, service clubs and philanthropic organizations, members of the Holiday Inn Select staff are involved in the community. The hotel is also generous in offering its services and facilities.

As Naperville continues to grow, the Holiday Inn Select has the facilities, quality and vision to continue providing outstanding service to travelers and businesses. Management's commitment to the community also ensures that Naperville's residents and service organizations will continue to benefit from its expertise and resources.

Holiday Inn Select
1801 Naper Boulevard
Naperville, IL 60563
630.505.4900
www.naperselect.com

The award-winning Holiday Inn Select Naperville has 426 guest rooms, including executive and parlor suites. Guests are pampered with amenities like coffee makers, irons and ironing boards, hair dryers, makeup mirrors, well-lit desk work areas, second phones with dataports, on-demand in-room movies, voice mail, free high-speed Internet access and an indoor pool and fitness center.

AT HOME IN THE *Heartland*

Neighborhood names such as Goose Pimple Heights, Pill Hill, Piety Hill and Stump Hill conjure up memories of growing up here for many natives and longtime residents. When the community began to expand outside the heart of downtown into the farmland, Naperville began to grow, one neighborhood at a time.

Somewhere along the way, the neighborhoods became known as subdivisions, developed by local builders. And today the community, from Aero Estates to Yorkshire, is organized as a big family of subdivisions with defining — and not-so-defining — names spread out over 37.6 square miles.

Back in 1949, entrepreneur Harold Moser began his first development, "The Forest Preserve," on the west side of downtown. A little better than half a century later, the community has grown in all directions to include some 180 subdivisions.

Moser left his mark, cashing in on the strong values in this faithful community where he is recognized for his lifetime achievement as a "community builder" in the suburbs. Moser's distinctive impact, in many ways similar to Joe Naper's 100 years before him, included generous support of community endeavors, a spirit which has caught on, as residents and businesses try to give back as much as they can to this exceptional city.

From a small commuter suburb in 1950 with a population of 7,000 residents, the community grew with Moser's innovative ideas into a place where people can work, live and enjoy many diverse cultural and sports activities right here at home.

During nearly 45 years as a community builder, Moser developed approximately 4,000 acres with about 10,000 home sites. And in 1994, the population passed 100,000.

In fact, according to tributes to Moser at his retirement party in 1994, he donated more than 200 acres to municipal officials for school sites, public parks, recreational areas, churches and other facilities.

Like Joe Naper, Moser, the successful businessman known as "Mr. Naperville," gave back to his community. Even today, successful businesses continue to emulate their pioneer spirit and willingness to contribute privately to education and community assets, partnering with local government entities to do it right.

As Naperville celebrates another milestone, the Naperville Area Homeowners' Confederation (NAHC) boasts 140 members.

Since 1981, when this umbrella organization was reorganized as a nonprofit and nonpolitical association, the NAHC has not only united subdivisions, but has also kept local residents within subdivisions connected and focused on good local government, parks and schools to benefit property values.

Just as in any organization, the confederation best serves its volunteer members when they become actively involved and recognize potential. Communication among member associations, homeowners and local officials enhances partnerships between the city and its constituents.

Through communication, networking and people helping people, the NAHC serves as a vehicle to monitor community affairs and generate a positive influence in determining the future of Naperville.

The group helps facilitate annual initiatives such as "Communities in Bloom" competitions with the Naperville Park District and "National Night Out" safety-awareness parties with the Naperville Police Department.

Everybody's welcome to participate in monthly meetings, candidates' forums during campaign seasons and occasional town hall meetings to foster an exchange of ideas and information between individual homeowners associations as well as individual homeowners.

In recent years, neighborhoods immediately surrounding downtown have begun to redevelop, probably much like the growth periods when log cabins were replaced by larger homes made from timber, bricks and stone. More and more, Naperville's housing market is producing bigger homes for evolving lifestyles.

Residents are attracted to downtown living within walking distance of Nichols Library, the Riverwalk, Kroehler YMCA, Alfred Rubin Center, Centennial Beach, Central Park, North Central College, Fifth Avenue Station, the commuter train, shopping and restaurants.

Over in the Historic District, gracious homes depicting a wide array of architectural styles from 1831 to 1920 line the blocks in the heart of the North Central College campus and north to Fifth Avenue Station.

In addition, every one of the city's subdivisions, whether north, south, east or west, has a unique character of its own — usually including a park and a nearby elementary school.

Thanks to the City of Naperville's land dedication ordinance, new developments will continue to donate land for parks.

With many new residential living concepts on the horizon — some designed to attract the senior adult community because so many folks are content to retire here — Naperville has no shortage of innovative and beautiful homes to complement good schools and neighborhood parks.

What's next? Pausing to reflect on the first 175 years evokes many questions regarding the future.

Who will be the next mayor? What's the next step? When will Naperville achieve build-out?

Where does Naperville want to be when the community celebrates its 200th anniversary in 2031?

How does a community best ensure that future generations participate and rejoice in the accomplishments of citizens eager to preserve one of the most desirable places to live in the United States?

Will the city maintain its status as one of the top communities in the nation to raise children, retire and start a home-based business?

As in the past, will Naperville's future support nationally acclaimed schools, the best public library system in the country and a remarkably low crime rate for a big city?

And who will be the next Mr. Naperville — or Ms. Naperville?

Many features define this community where service organizations, local business leaders and individuals work together to enhance the quality of life. And that's why new residents and business owners continually are attracted to move here and call Naperville home.

Tree-shaded sidewalks provide the perfect path for private strolls to ponder the future along the friendly public streets. Bicyclists still hug the roadside, and signs caution motorists to 'Drive 25 mph!' unless otherwise posted.

Gracious homes depicting the variety of architectural styles from 1830 to 1920 line the blocks of the historic district, centered in the heart of the North Central College campus and extending north to Fifth Avenue Station, formerly the Kroehler Manufacturing Company.

The Naperville Historic District and Naper Settlement attract history buffs for study and walking tours.

Roughly bounded by Julian, Highland, Chicago, Jackson and Eagle streets and Fifth Avenue to the north, the Naperville Historic District provides a fascinating backdrop to learn about Naperville history and North Central College. The showcase of homes throughout the neighborhoods provides fine examples of Prairie School, Greek Revival and Italianate architecture.

Naper Settlement, located several blocks south, just across from the Naperville Municipal Center, is unlike some historic outdoor museums set in a specific time period. The sampling of diverse architecture at Naper Settlement — from a pioneer log house to a Victorian mansion — provides a valuable exercise through changing times.

The Martin Mitchell Mansion, built as Pine Craig in 1883, is located at Naper Settlement and is listed on both the national and Illinois registers of historic places.

In 1936, more than 30 years before the grassroots initiative of the Naperville Heritage Society took hold, Caroline Martin Mitchell laid the groundwork for Naper Settlement by donating her family's Victorian mansion and the surrounding 212 acres to the City of Naperville. One of her requests was that her home would remain a museum in perpetuity. Today, the interior and exterior of her home exhibit their original Victorian splendor, due to a three-year, $2.8 million restoration project completed in 2003.

Mounds of **rich black dirt** create a **dusting of progress**

during every construction season. With visions of

Naperville Crossings and **Carriage Club of Naperville**

at 95th Street and Route 59, other developments,

such as **English Rows** near 111th Street and the

Carillon Club south of **White Eagle**, offer lifestyle

choices for empty nesters and senior citizens.

First-time homeowners, empty nesters and senior citizens find quality housing along every tree-lined street. New and established subdivisions with single-family homes, residential communities with state-of-the-art amenities, and downtown condominiums near the thriving business center offer choices for every lifestyle imaginable.

> "I've never done a cookie-cutter development. Each subdivision has had its own identity, and that's what has set us apart through the years and affected the character of the community."
>
> **— Harold Moser**

Since 1956, Aero Estates has been another of Naperville's unique neighborhoods. Not only do many of the spacious homes have swimming pools, but all the homes are situated near Aero Estates Club Field, a small private airport with a runway and taxi areas. And the giant garages outside the back door are hangars for private aircraft!

The Lima Lima Flight Team has been based at Aero Estates Club Field since 1975. The award-winning precision-formation flying squadron is a familiar sight overhead during Memorial Day parades, Veterans Day services and other patriotic events. Residents even receive a spectacular air show when the squadron practices.

During the last frontier of new development, builders continue to enhance the picturesque landscape with neighborhoods featuring a healthy blend of classic architectural styles and innovative design.

Historic downtown Naperville has been revitalized by redevelopment and reinvestment. Today, the Van Buren Parking Deck, Van Buren Place, Washington Place and Main Street Promenade attract a new set of businesses, restaurants and customers.

Adjacent to the Main Street Promenade, just to the north, Benton Place will house 21 luxury condominiums. All the amenities of the thriving downtown are attracting residents to other upscale downtown housing on the rise, too.

NAPERVILLE AREA HUMANE SOCIETY

Founded in 1979, the Naperville Area Humane Society is much more than an animal shelter and placement agency. This outstanding organization also serves the entire region with much-needed programs and services that benefit not only the animals, but also the people of the community.

The Naperville Area Humane Society works to develop and implement animal welfare programs and services. While the society's primary mission is always to protect animals and prevent animal suffering, its staff, Board, members and volunteers also strive daily to educate the community about compassion toward all living things. The society's ultimate goal is to end the cycle of violence toward people and animals.

Providing shelter and placing animals in new homes is the most familiar way the society works to achieve this goal; but this award-winning organization goes even further to safeguard the welfare of people and animals. The Naperville Area Humane Society offers the city's only Multi-Tiered Humane Education program for children, at-risk youth, and those with behavior disorders and autism. Carefully designed to teach humane values, these programs include discussions on animal communication, dog and cat handling, veterinary care, and dog training. Each class gives participants the opportunity to gain hands-on experience in caring for animals.

The society also extends compassion to the people of our community, making over 40 pet therapy visits per month to local hospitals and convalescent centers. And the society is proud to offer the community a foster program for the pets of domestic violence victims, a crisis care program for hospital staff who work around the clock, a behavior modification program, a 24-hour help line, and discounted spay/neuter services.

For their efforts, the society has been recognized with several awards, including honorable mention for Excellence in Education from the Chicago Veterinary Medical Association, the Distinguished Service Award from the Naperville Jaycees, and the Award for Business Excellence from *The Business Ledger*.

These programs would not be possible without the financial support and volunteer efforts of the community. Over 400 volunteers and a membership base numbering over 100 daily help carry out the society's important work. To receive more information about the society and its programs, to inquire about adopting a pet, or to volunteer to donate time or financial assistance, please contact the Naperville Area Humane Society today. With your help, we can ensure a bright future for the people and animals of this great community.

Naperville Area Humane Society
1620 W. Diehl Road
Naperville, IL 60563
630.420.8989
napervillehumanesociety.org

[top] The Naperville Area Humane Society's shelter will soon be supplemented by a 10,000-square-foot center for children and animals.

[bottom] Adopting a new member of the family is one of life's most joyous events.

Blossoms blanket the landscape every spring.

JACKSON MOVING & STORAGE

From office moves and employee relocations to families moving down the block, around the country or overseas, Jackson Moving & Storage has been the top pick in the Naperville and Chicagoland area since 1888. Known for their "customer first" service, Jackson will take the stress out of your moving day.

As a founding member of Allied Van Lines in 1928, Jackson has been consistently recognized for high-quality service, receiving the Customer for Life Service award in 2004 — Allied's top quality award.

Jackson is currently located in an 110,000-square-foot warehouse on North Aurora Road, just west of the Route 59 Metra station. Jackson moved out of the All Seasons Ice Arena in 2000, to allow that facility to expand.

Jackson Moving & Storage offers a full range of moving and storage services, including:

- Local and In-State Household Moves
- State-to-State Moves
- Employee Relocations
- International Relocations
- Office/Commercial Moving
- Residential/Commercial and Record Storage
- Product Distribution and Warehousing

Jackson's core values recognize that it is important to be involved in the community. Jackson demonstrates this commitment by supporting the Naperville and Metro Chicago United Ways, the Naperville Area Chamber of Commerce, School District #203, Naperville Park District, Magical Starlight Theatre, YMCA, Boy Scouts, Ray Graham, North Central College, and Naper Days. All of these great organizations make Naperville a great place to live and do business, and Jackson Moving & Storage is honored to be associated with them.

Call today for a free estimate and to experience Jackson's "customer first" service.

Jackson Moving & Storage
740 Frontenac Road
Naperville, IL 60563
630.357.4400
www.JacksonMoving.com
insidesales@jacksonmoving.com

Jackson Moving & Storage has been the number-one choice among moving companies in the Chicagoland area since 1888.

Calamos Investments
2020 Calamos Court
Naperville, IL 60563
630.245.7200
www.calamos.com

CALAMOS INVESTMENTS:
AT HOME IN NAPERVILLE

When Calamos Investments opened its doors 27 years ago, it was in the heart of Chicago's financial district on LaSalle Street. Like many other companies, Calamos migrated to the western suburbs, moving into its original Naperville headquarters on Warrenville Road in 1994. Then, Calamos was a boutique investment manager specializing in convertible securities for institutions and high net worth individuals. Today, Calamos is one of the industry's leading money managers, with over $38 billion in assets under management and serving over one million investors and their financial advisors.

"Reflecting back, the growth of Naperville and the growth of our business have been on very similar paths" says Chairman, CEO and founder John P. Calamos, Sr. "Our success is a byproduct of performing well for our clients.

We remain dedicated to providing them with best-in-class money management strategies. Our growth has come and will continue to come from expanding and deepening our client base."

John Calamos' interest in investing began at an early age. As a teenager, he successfully invested $5,000 of his family's saving, and his fascination grew. With an undergraduate degree in Economics and MBA in Finance from the Illinois Institute of Technology, John joined the United States Air Force, serving as a combat pilot during the Viet Nam war and ultimately earning the rank of Major. During the turbulent 1970s, John demonstrated success at the use of convertible bonds to help manage risk. In fact, the Calamos proprietary investment process grew out of its roots as a convertible bond boutique.

We choose to grow our business in Naperville because it is an outstanding community for our business and for our employees. It offers convenient access for our business partners, a great pool of talent, a wonderful community for our employees to work and live in.

As the company grew, John's nephew, Nick Calamos, joined the firm, computerizing and enhancing the Calamos proprietary investment process. Later his son, John Jr. also came aboard. Together, they lead the company's portfolio management, which takes a team-based approach on delivering value-added performance. Calamos has built a record of excellent performance across an array of investment strategies ranging from conservative to aggressive, all built upon the common foundation of valuing companies.

"We are first and foremost risk managers. While other investment firms talk about risk management, Calamos has always seen preservation of capital as a key component of creating wealth and we have the track record to support it." says Nick P. Calamos, Co-Chief Investment Officer.

In mid-2005, Calamos moved its headquarters to its new 150,000 square-foot facility at the intersection of I-88 and Route 59. Just as Calamos advises its clients to invest for the long-term, Calamos took a long-term view of the firm's needs and growth and developed a new facility designed by renowned Chicago architect, Dirk Lohan of Lohan Anderson with state-of-the-art technology and environmental efficiency.

Calamos Investment's headquarters is designed with state-of-the-art technology to access markets around the world and manage portfolios on a global basis.

The new Calamos Investments' headquarters incorporates employee amenities, state-of-the-art technology and sustainable design elements. This environmentally friendly, "green building" approach makes it one of the first privately developed buildings in the Chicago area to be registered with the U.S. Green Building Council for Leadership in Energy and Environmental Design (LEED) certification.

Calamos Investments is truly a family business. Founder, Chairman, CEO and Co-Chief Investment Officer, John P. Calamos, Sr., center, is joined by his son, John P. Calamos, Jr. left and his nephew, Nick P. Calamos, Co-Chief Investment Officer, right.

The new Calamos Investments' headquarters incorporates employee amenities, state-of-the-art technology and sustainable design elements. This environmentally friendly, "green building" approach makes it one of the first privately developed buildings in the Chicago area to be registered with the U.S. Green Building Council for Leadership in Energy and Environmental Design (LEED) certification.

From the clang of metal upon metal in the Blacksmith Shop to the soft rustle of long gowns at the Victorian-era Martin Mitchell Mansion, a visit to the past is never far away when you step onto the grounds of Naper Settlement. More than 30 historic businesses, homes and buildings can be found at the 13-acre living history museum, located one block south of the Riverwalk in downtown Naperville. Drawing upon the rich history of northern Illinois, the past comes to life through the interpretation of costumed villagers who tell the story of how Naperville, and Midwestern towns like it, changed from frontier outposts to bustling turn-of-the-century communities.

With its beautiful landscaping and numerous period structures, the Naper Settlement of today is very different from its fledgling start in 1969. At that time, a courageous group of citizens banded together to save St. John's Episcopal Church from possible demolition and formed the Naperville Heritage Society. They raised money and moved the church to a site owned by the City of Naperville, situated on land close to the Martin Mitchell Mansion. The church, which was the first major structure relocated to what would become Naper Settlement, was restored to its Civil War-era appearance and renamed Century Memorial Chapel.

The mansion at the top of the hill was the home of Caroline Martin Mitchell, who donated it and the 212 surrounding acres of land to the city. When Caroline died in 1936, her bequest was left with two stipulations: that her home be used as a city museum and that the land be used for public good. Since 1939, the elegant mansion, listed on the National Register of Historic Places, has been open to the public. From 2000 to 2003, the mansion underwent a $2.8 million restoration, which has garnered numerous state and national awards and restored the Victorian beauty to its former glory.

Through the years, the Naperville Heritage Society, which administers Naper Settlement, has been an enthusiastic advocate for preservation in the community. From its humble beginnings, Naper Settlement has grown into a nationally recognized institution, receiving accreditation from the American Association of Museums in 2002.

Today, more than 150,000 visitors annually, from nearby and around the globe, visit Naper Settlement. Of those, more than 35,000 schoolchildren attend field trips throughout the school year to experience what living history is all about.

In addition to the buildings and grounds, Naper Settlement is also the repository of more than 23,000 objects, archival materials and over 4,200 photographs related to local history. A fascinating collection of 42 folk art paintings created by local artist Lester E. Schrader is the basis of the interactive exhibit titled, "Brushstrokes of the Past … Naperville's Story," located in the Pre-Emption House.

With help from its friends in the community, the devotion of a dedicated group of volunteers and the commitment of a staff that numbers more than 50, Naper Settlement is a living history museum with its roots firmly in the past, but its branches reaching out to the future as it continues to grow and flourish to celebrate many more anniversaries.

Naper Settlement
A Living History Village
523 South Webster Street
Naperville, Illinois 60540
630.420.6010
www.napersettlement.museum

The 13-acre village comes to life during the summer season. Visitors may enter the buildings and meet costumed interpreters who will share the experiences of daily life, work and celebration in a 19th century Midwestern town.

Naper Settlement's unique school programs give students a lesson in Northern Illinois heritage that they can't get out of any textbook — because here in the village, history lessons come alive, with sights and sounds at every turn recreating the 19th century.

john greene, Realtor
1311 South Route 59
Naperville, IL 60564
630.229.2200
johngreenerealtor.com

I n 1976, John Greene founded his vision of an innovative real estate company staffed by talented, highly trained real estate agents and guided by a commitment to providing unparalleled service to their clients and their community. John Greene wanted his agents to sell real estate in "… a better way" — thus creating the motto that has defined john greene, Realtor for more than 29 years.

Even if you have never done business with john greene, Realtor, you have probably heard of the company's numerous sponsorships, educational events and other community connections. It is this dedication to community that makes john greene, Realtor more than a successful Naperville real estate firm; it is an integral part of Naperville and everything it is today.

At the core of john greene, Realtor's success are three simple philosophies: teamwork, education and community service.

TEAMWORK

Ask any john greene, Realtor agent what makes the company unique, and he or she will tell you it is the Team philosophy — the idea that the whole is truly more than the sum of its parts. The use of lowercase letters in the company's name is intended to de-emphasize the person and focus on the Team. In an industry that is traditionally competitive, territorial and focused on the individual, john greene, Realtor offers a refreshing change in that each agent is genuinely concerned for the success of each agent and the Team as a whole.

Everyone who buys or sells a home with john greene, Realtor has the support of a highly trained and knowledge-able agent and the backing of 130 team members who are committed to the success of each client, each agent, their entire company and their entire community.

TRAINING

john greene, Realtor agents, regardless of experience, are trained extensively on company philosophies, sales techniques, listing strategies, ethics and community information. In addition, new agents are involved in mentoring programs with more experienced john greene, Realtor agents until they are fully acclimated to the firm, the market and the community.

The learning does not stop when the initial training is over. All john greene, Realtor agents attend professional development workshops several times a year. john greene, Realtor prides itself on the number of professional designations that their agents have attained through education in the industry.

COMMUNITY SERVICE

A key to the success of john greene, Realtor is its commitment to staying an intergral part of the community. This core value states that when you work and live in a community, it is your responsibility to give back to it.

New agents expand their knowledge of this great community through area tours, and many attend the Naperville Area Chamber of Commerce Leadership Program. All agents are encouraged to become involved in service clubs, churches, charities and schools, as well as with professional organizations. The john greene, Realtor Team supports over 50 professional and community events and organizations and

is especially dedicated to supporting education. The company has active business-education partnerships with the Naperville and Indian Prairie School Districts and hosts Excellence in Education banquets for top students at all four Naperville High Schools and Oswego High School.

john greene, Realtor is proud to be Naperville's "Hometown Realtor" and looks forward to many more years of active service to clients and the community.

AWARDS

- 2005 Award for Business Excellence (*The Business Ledger*)
- 2004 Naperville Area Chamber of Commerce Small Business of the Year
- 2003 Testimonial Award for Outstanding and Devoted Service
- 2002 Employees Relocation Council (ERC) Meritorious Service Award
- Annual RELO Service Awards since 1985
- Sam Walton Business Leader Award, John Schmitt

"john greene, Realtor is one of those exceptional companies that cares deeply about the communities they serve. They have played an instrumental role in our economic development program and continue to lend their expertise to assist our businesses to grow and new residents to feel welcome. Keep up the great work!"

Christine Jeffries
Naperville Development Partnership

john greene, Realtor was honored as the Naperville Area Chamber of Commerce's Small Business of the Year for 2004. Here, John Schmitt (L), President of john greene, Realtor, and Naperville Mayor A. George Pradel (R) pose with the award.

First National Bank of Naperville
555 Fort Hill Drive
Naperville, IL 60540
630.369.3555
www.FNBNaperville.com

Whether mortgages, business loans or car loans, First National Bank of Naperville is here to be involved with all the new growth that makes this city so youthful, exciting and successful.

FIRST NATIONAL BANK OF NAPERVILLE — YOUR FRIENDLY HOMETOWN COMMUNITY BANK.

In this day and age when most banks are big — and being bought out by even bigger banking institutions — the First National Bank of Naperville promises to be your community bank.

Though our history in Naperville began after the new millennium, our spirited mission captures the friendliness, values and traditions that started here in 1831. We still take care of mom and pop businesses and personal banking, just as those commonplace needs were managed 175 years ago in downtown Naperville. We'll always be hands-on to meet your financial requests.

When the quality of life in Naperville and the community's dedication to families first caught our eye, we knew Naperville would be a fun place to own a bank. As a rising star and Illinois' fourth-largest city, we saw Naperville's growth and devotion to community as the perfect place for our family, too.

We'd been in the family banking business for about 40 years, experiencing great success and growth in Brookfield. More and more, our business associates and friends had connections to Naperville. We found ourselves visiting North Central College for sporting events, as well as for dining and shopping in downtown. We loved the Riverwalk. We felt at home. We could not resist the opportunity we discovered here — like so many other business men and women before us.

In November 2002 we began meetings with the City of Naperville, following the process for the approval to bring our bank here.

In January 2003, First National Bank of Brookfield purchased the land for what we now affectionately call our "international headquarters."

A few months later we joined the Naperville Area Chamber of Commerce, and the Chamber's been with us every step of the way, from our groundbreaking to our ribbon cutting to our grand opening.

Along the way, our son, Brian Schultz, joined our family business, and we named him President of the First National Bank of Naperville. In June 2003, Brian jumped in with both feet running.

With a slogan, "The art of banking," we lent our name to sponsor the Riverwalk Fine Arts Fair, the DuPage Symphony Orchestra and Naper Days at Naper Settlement.

While our beautiful new bank was under construction, Brian opened a satellite branch in the shopping center nearby.

The first full-service branch of the First National Bank of Naperville was ready in the summer of 2004.

Tragically, Brian was killed by a drunk driver in Chicago on New Year's Day 2005. We can't tell our story without expressing our gratitude for the incredible outpouring of kindnesses we've found in this community.

Beginning every deal with a firm handshake, Brian always hoped to send the right message about community banking and trust. We owe it to Brian to continue the legacy he started.

> *"We want to do smart business with you."*

Whether mortgages, business loans or car loans, we're here to be involved with all the new growth that makes this city so youthful, exciting and successful.

As your hometown community bank, our dreams include other convenient locations to serve all of Naperville. In the meantime, we will remain dedicated to your financial future and your friendship.

VISIT OUR BANK AND ATM PLAZA LOCATED AT 555 FORT HILL DRIVE AND AURORA AVENUE IN NAPERVILLE.

MESSAGE FROM PEGGY AND JAN SCHULTZ

"Never have a bad day."
— *Brian R. Schultz*
June 15, 1976–January 1, 2005

When someone is killed by a drunk driver, it's no accident. It's the result of a fatal choice of someone who got behind the wheel of a car after drinking too much alcohol. Just like our son Brian, too many good, beautiful young people have their innovative ideas and bright futures taken away because someone made the deadly decision to drink and drive. For a decade, the skillful Naperville police force has been increasingly committed toward keeping drunk drivers off the road. We applaud them. Drive safe. Drive sober. Don't make a mistake that could cost lives or ruin yours.

Nicor Gas is known for its safe, reliable and economical delivery of natural gas service to its more than two million customers in northern Illinois.

Established in 1954, Nicor Gas is a company with roots in the farmlands of northern Illinois, serving more than 640 communities. Our underground storage system is among the largest in the industry, enabling us to meet roughly one-third of our annual deliveries with gas from storage. In addition, access to multiple pipelines gives us the flexibility to provide customers with competitively priced natural gas supplies while ensuring reliable gas delivery year round.

HISTORICAL BACKGROUND

Nicor Gas celebrated 50 years of service in 2004, but our company roots actually date back to 1855 to the Ottawa Gas Light and Coke Company, which lit the historic Lincoln-Douglas debate in Ottawa on August 21, 1858. In the late 1800s, natural gas was produced from coal and transported short distances through hollow wooden logs. However, by the early 1900s, 4-inch steel pipe was used to transport natural gas locally, and 76 gas companies had sprung up in Illinois, serving customers in 229 towns.

At this time, Commonwealth Edison owned several gas and electric utilities, but as concerns surrounding the technical and operating differences between the utilities increased, gas properties were transferred to a newly organized company on February 9, 1954 — Northern Illinois Gas.

EARLY BEGINNINGS

As a young company during the postwar boom, Northern Illinois Gas served 479,000 customers and added new customers at a staggering rate of one every four minutes! With all these customers, we had to make sure there was enough gas available for everyone, so in 1957, we began work with geologists to establish our own storage system.

While northern Illinois doesn't have sandy beaches or mountain views, what it does have are vast underground sandstone formations, which proved to be perfect for storing natural gas. Taking full advantage of this geology, we established our first storage field in Troy Grove in July 1958.

A GROWING COMPANY

By 1972, Nicor Gas owned and operated seven underground storage fields in Illinois, enhancing our ability to serve customers without interruption. Our Ancona storage field, established in 1965, is today the single largest storage field in the country, both in acreage and storage capacity.

Our service territory expanded west in 1970 when we acquired Mid-Illinois Gas Company. This was our largest acquisition, making Northern Illinois Gas the largest distribution utility in Illinois and one of the largest gas distributors in the nation. Nicor Inc. was

(TOP)
Nicor Gas owns, operates and maintains more than 28,000 miles of pipe in its underground natural gas delivery system. Additionally, the company adds 30,000 new customers to its system annually.

(BOTTOM)
Nicor Gas' roots date back to the 1850s, when the Ottawa Gas Light and Coke Company provided lighting for the historic Lincoln–Douglas debate in Ottawa.

The company has taken full advantage of northern Illinois' vast underground sand formations for storing natural gas. The company's first storage field was established in Troy Grove in July 1958.

Nicor Gas' headquarters is located in Naperville, Illinois. The company serves more than 2 million customers in 640 communities across nothern Illinois.

formed as a holding company in 1976, with Northern Illinois Gas operating as its principal subsidiary.

The first major gas-fired cogeneration plant in our service territory began producing electricity in 1985, and by the mid-1990s, gas-fired electric generation was one of our biggest developing markets.

> *Nicor Gas is known for its safe, reliable and economical delivery of natural gas service.*

EXPANDING THE ENERGY BUSINESS

Nicor Gas opened the Chicago Hub in 1993, the first market-area hub in the United States to be owned and operated by a local distribution company. In 1997, the Illinois Commerce Commission approved a three-year pilot program for Customer Select, a natural gas supplier choice program, which was later expanded to all customers in 2001. Also in 1997, we changed our name to Nicor Gas as part of our overall plan to promote the "Nicor" brand and unify our presence in the energy marketplace.

Today, Nicor Gas is a company well-situated for continued progress — our service territory, customer mix and operating expertise remain strong factors in ensuring our position as one of the nation's leading natural gas distribution utilities.

BUILDING A BETTER COMMUNITY

Nicor Gas has been part of the Northern Illinois landscape for more than 50 years, and we have a strong commitment to the economic growth of this area. Nicor Gas provides both financial and human resources to municipal and regional economic development organizations. Additionally, in 2004 Nicor Gas and its employees contributed more than $1.8 million to philanthropic efforts throughout northern Illinois. The company's employees joined with community members to donate their time, talent and money to 825 worthy causes throughout the year, further growing the company's philanthropic mission and commitment to volunteer efforts.

Nicor Gas
1844 Ferry Road
Naperville, IL 60563
630.388.2689
www.nicorgas.com

A LIFETIME OF
Learning

 very monumental anniversary is a time of reflection and celebration, hoping to ensure that future generations participate and rejoice in the accomplishments of hometown Naperville.

Naperville's historic mission to educate was recorded in detailed diaries written by Hannah Ditzler Alspaugh. Born in 1848, Alspaugh embraced students with her knowledge at Naper Academy, both as a classmate and a teacher.

Today, two large public school districts, the Naperville Community Unit School District 203 and the Indian Prairie Unit School District 204, serve the needs of students with boundaries running from north to south.

Naperville's graduates have become leaders in small and big business, medicine, international trade, paleontology, architecture, engineering, literature, journalism, performing arts and television news, as well as in local, county, state and federal government.

With 56 acres nestled in Naperville's Historic District, just a couple of blocks from a happening downtown, North Central College has reserved the right to be known as Naperville's college since 1870.

Early trustees of the college were enticed to move to Naperville just nine years after North Central's founding in Plainfield. Citizens agree that the $25,000 raised for the move was some of the best private money ever collected.

In recent years, Naperville has been similarly successful in attracting new institutions of private and public learning.

On the occasion of its 175th year, Naperville is certain to pay tribute to the countless individuals over the decades and centuries who have given their hearts and souls to make this milestone possible. This city's schools are worthy of celebration by both Naperville natives and newcomers, people who value and support education and all that's been accomplished here since 1831.

Fully aware that resting on one's laurels leads only to stagnation, local and school officials are always on the move to better the city's educational opportunities and resources.

Citizens continually renew their purpose with volunteer initiatives and a dedication to high ideals and quality of life that benefit all the city's institutions of learning.

Whether public, private, parochial or home-school, education for Naperville's youth and adult community is always a top priority.

"Since the first one-room schoolhouse was built in 1832, Naperville continually has received high marks as a center of education, research and development."

Nearly **19 years** after his arrival, Captain **Joe Naper** donated land and stone from his quarry to begin **Naper Academy** in 1850. The **three-story school** opened in 1852.

Photo by Jeffery Ross

Naperville's oldest school was demolished and rebuilt in 1928. The new school is today's Naper School. The new millennium brought a new addition to the south side of the building. The bell tower from the original school continues to ring out to tell students it's time for school.

Education has always received high marks in Naperville. From nursery schools to adult education at local colleges and universities, highly educated parents send their children to strong schools to instill a desire for lifelong learning in preparation for college.

Naperville Community Unit School District 203 and Indian Prairie Unit School District 204 offer high academic standards and a wide range of extracurricular activities along with gifted and special-needs programs. District 204, the state's fastest-growing school district, serves the southwest area, which is still under development.

Pie-eating contests are as much for the spectators as the contestants during Naper Days, a three-day festival jam-packed with old-fashioned games, live entertainment and family fun on Father's Day Weekend.

Naperville's two area school districts support kindergarten through grade 12, five high schools, champion athletes and sports teams, and nationally recognized science, math, music and arts programs.

Always mobilized with community support for excellent education, Naperville parents push for recreational opportunities and good health care to give kids a well-balanced advantage on many fronts.

On average, a Naperville resident checks out more than 25 items in a year, making Naperville's three full-service public libraries active centers of the community.

In fact, from May 2003 to April 2004, NPL checked out nearly 3.5 million (3,447,044) books, videos, CDs and other materials, a 16 percent increase from the previous year. Who knows what tomorrow will bring!

**Naperville
Community Unit
School District 203**
203 W. Hillside Road
Naperville, IL 60540
630.420.6300
www.ncusd203.org

**Indian Prairie
School District 204**
780 Shoreline Drive
Aurora, IL 60504
630.375.3000
www.ipsd.org

Naperville is fortunate to have two internationally-recognized public school districts educating the young people of our community. Naperville Community Unit School District 203 and Indian Prairie School District 204 consistently rank among the highest-scoring school districts in the country on standardized test scores, and eighth-graders in District 203 ranked first in the world in science on the Third International Mathematics and Science Study Repeat (TIMSS-R) and sixth in math. Both districts have been recognized for providing top-quality educations while responsibly and efficiently using tax dollars.

District 203 came into being in 1972 when Naperville High School District 107 and Naperville Elementary District 78 consolidated. Naperville North High opened its doors in 1975, joining Naperville (Central) High at the district's highest level. With some 20,000 students and 1,300+ teachers at its 21 schools, District 203 includes much of Naperville, parts of Lisle, and areas in Bolingbrook, Warrenville and Woodridge.

District 204, the fourth-largest system in the state of Illinois, was also formed through consolidation in 1972 and includes parts of Naperville, Aurora, Bolingbrook and Plainfield in DuPage and Will Counties. Its 31 schools (as of 2005) serve more than 26,000 students and employ nearly 2,000 educators.

Naperville's educational system has kept pace with the community's growth from its 19th-century, agrarian roots to a leader in the 21st century, and continues to add to the quality of life here.

The schools of both District 203 and District 204 are consistent leaders in high academic achievement across the country.

A **well-rounded** approach to learning prepares students for more **demanding** **expectations** at the collegiate level, which helps students **excel** in both school and life.

Nestled in Naperville's historic district, North Central College has reserved the right to be known as Naperville's college since 1870, when folks in Naperville enticed college trustees to move the small liberal arts college from Plainfield just nine years after its founding.

Today, North Central College is an independent, comprehensive college of the liberal arts and sciences affiliated with the United Methodist Church. In 2005, enrollment was slightly more than 2,500 students, including some 1,770 full-time undergraduates and over 750 part-time undergraduate and graduate students.

North Central is nationally known for the quality of its faculty and students. Consistently recognized as one of "America's Best Colleges" by *U.S. News & World Report*, North Central is ranked among the "top choices for top students" by *Peterson's Competitive Colleges* and is among a select number of schools profiled in *Kaplan's Unofficial Insider's Guide to the 320 Most Interesting Colleges*.

North Central College
30 N. Brainard St.
Naperville, IL 60540
630.637.5100
www.northcentralcollege.edu

NORTH CENTRAL COLLEGE ...
WHERE YOU ARE CENTRAL

Photos courtesy of North Central College

North Central College is "Naperville's College" and has been for seven generations ... with deep roots in a community that has grown from a modest 19th century farming village to today's "second city to the Second City."

The College has developed too, from a small school founded in 1861 by Evangelical Christians and dedicated mainly to the education of "teachers and preachers," into one of the finest comprehensive liberal arts institutions in the nation, affiliated with the United Methodist Church and offering values-based education that encompasses the arts, humanities, sciences, social sciences and pre-professional disciplines.

For over a decade, *U.S. News & World Report* has consistently ranked North Central in the top 10 percent of Midwest colleges and universities. *Peterson's Competitive Colleges* includes the school among an elite list of institutions that "routinely attract and admit an above-average share of the nation's high achieving students." Students win prestigious graduate fellowships — Goldwater, Soros, Fulbright, Howard Hughes — and faculty, 90 percent of whom have the highest degree in their discipline, hold Ph.D.'s from pre-eminent universities.

ACCLAIMED ACADEMICS

(TOP)
North Central College is situated on a beautiful 56-acre campus adjoining the Naperville Historic District in the heart of downtown Naperville. Much of "life" happens in the campus residence halls, dining facilities, the coffeehouse, recreational facilities and other favorite student hangouts.

With strengths across the curriculum, and a nationally acclaimed focus on interdisciplinary education, the College offers bachelor's degrees in more than 50 majors. North Central is also well known in its co-curricular activities, with nationally distinguished forensics, radio and Students In Free Enterprise programs, and more national athletic championships than all but a handful of NCAA Division III institutions. A charter member of the Associated New American Colleges, a national association of 20 "best in class" comprehensive colleges, North Central blends the highly personalized qualities of a liberal arts college with the diversity of a large university.

The College serves 2,500 students, including 1,800 full-time undergraduates, 1,000 of whom live in the residence halls. Another 700 students attend classes part-time in the evenings or on weekends to complete an undergraduate degree or participate in one of six master's degree programs. Students of high school age, and occasionally even younger, may also be seen on campus, enrolled in special programs that offer highly motivated youth the opportunity to earn College credit while still in school.

North Central takes advantage of its closeness (two blocks) to the Metra commuter train to Chicago with an innovative Chicago Term that gives the College's students a taste of the many facets of that great city. They are also encouraged to immerse themselves in a culture other than their own. They can choose 10-week North Central programs in London, Costa Rica and China/Japan; exchange programs with schools in Korea, Taiwan, Northern Ireland, France, China, Japan, England and Sweden; direct enrollment in programs in the United Kingdom, Ireland, Australia, Ghana and Germany; or shorter travel seminars during the three-week Interim Term.

The College's graduates can be found working throughout the United States and around the globe, as doctors, attorneys, business leaders, entrepreneurs, social workers, artists, scientists, public servants and in a host of other professions ... including as dedicated teachers and preachers.

WORLD-CLASS LOCATION

But Naperville is home, a city that's been described as one of the "best places to live in America." It's a draw for students, parents, faculty and staff alike. And North Central likes to return the favor. From the day the College relocated to Naperville from Plainfield in 1870 at the invitation of the city's civic leaders, it has been central to the success and growth of this dynamic community.

North Central has been Naperville's cultural hub, bringing visitors such as Helen Keller, Robert Frost, Carl Sandburg, Dr. Martin Luther King Jr. and Marian Wright Edelman to the city and, with the construction of Pfeiffer Hall in 1926, hundreds of major artists, from Harry Belafonte and Carol Channing to Gregory Hines and Judy Collins.

The College is a major player in the vitality and excitement of downtown Naperville ... hosting the Chicago Fire professional soccer club at magnificent 5,500-seat Benedetti-Wehrli Stadium for two seasons ... offering NCAA Division III play just about every weekend, along with regional, state and national high school and college championships ... planning a soon-to-be-built first-class concert hall and fine arts center to serve both students and the community ... and providing, through its students, much of the workforce for the more than 50 restaurants and hundreds of stores within a few blocks of the campus.

Alumni have served as Naperville mayors and school superintendents; and it's hard to find a Naperville school whose quality doesn't rest, at least in part, on the talents of North Central's education graduates. In the civic arena in recent years, faculty and staff have included the head of the Naperville Planning Commission and the founding chair of the Naperville Development Partnership.

SUCCESSFUL ALUMNI

Illustrious alumni of North Central go all the way back to Frederick L. Maytag, class of 1876, founder of the company that bears his name, and Egyptologist James Henry Breasted, class of 1890, who established the internationally renowned Oriental Institute at the University of Chicago, right up to Harold and Eva White, class of 1935, publishers of Naperville's newspaper for 50 years, Mildred Rebstock, class of 1942, nominated for a Nobel Prize for her scientific achievements, and Bob Wislow, class of 1967, CEO of the development firm with a prime responsibility for such Chicago landmarks as the Harold Washington Library and the new Millennium Park, to name only a few.

Perhaps there's a future James Henry Breasted or Mildred Rebstock among contemporary graduates. Time will tell. But one thing is certain. At North Central College, students ... and community ... are central. There are few colleges anywhere that can compete with North Central's location. The pride the school feels in its city is matched by the pride the people of Naperville have in the College that has been such an important part of Naperville's success in three centuries.

(TOP)
North Central views athletics as a training ground for developing great people who know what it means to go after a goal and to work as part of a team. North Central is the only school in the CCIW to win national championships in four different sports. The Cardinals have won 18 National Collegiate Athletic Association (NCAA) national titles and four National Intercollegiate Athletic Association (NAIA) national titles.

(BOTTOM)
North Central faculty choose to be at a place where teaching and students come first. The college looks for people with a passion for small-group, hands-on instruction. A 14-to-1 undergraduate student-to-faculty ratio and small class sizes allow students and faculty mentors to develop a bond of trust and friendship that often extends far beyond graduation.

Innovative hands-on

experiences inspire

curiosity while providing

a fun way to learn at the

DuPage Children's Museum,

fostering the pursuit

of lifelong education.

WILLIAM J. CARROLL, PH.D.

William J. Carroll, Ph.D., became the 10th president of Benedictine University in July 1995. Under Carroll's leadership many new initiatives have begun, and he has been instrumental in the transformation of Benedictine University to a regional institution.

The Great Issues-Great Ideas Lecture Series, now in its 10th year, is an issues-oriented program, providing thought-provoking lectures and discussions regarding the state of the Union, race, peace and adventures in space by bonafide American heroes, prominent world leaders and inspirational religious personalities.

Master's degree programs and a doctoral program were introduced, and the Rev. Dr. Martin Luther King Jr. Day Breakfast, now in its ninth year, began during Carroll's tenure. New campus facilities include Kindlon Hall of Learning, Birck Hall of Science, Founders' Woods apartments and the newly completed Sports Complex.

Carroll was instrumental in forming a partnership with the Lisle-Woodridge Fire District, participating in fire training, offering a campus building as a training facility, and establishing a scholarship program where firefighters can earn a college degree by taking classes at fire stations.

Benedictine University formed a partnership in 2003 with Springfield College in Illinois, providing junior-senior level classes and graduate programs in the state capital.

Benedictine University was founded by the Benedictine monks of St. Procopius Abbey in 1887. Today, Benedictine enrolls more than 2,100 undergraduates and more than 1,000 graduate students.

Benedictine University sits on beautiful, tree-filled land in Lisle, Illinois, just 25 miles west of Chicago. Benedictine provides 42 undergraduate majors, eight graduate programs and a world-renowned Ph.D. in Organization Development. Benedictine has repeatedly been named one of the top schools in the Midwest region and is ranked seventh in the Midwest for Campus Diversity by *U.S. News & World Report.*

Benedictine's academic excellence, abundant opportunities and strong student/teacher relationship help students realize their full potential. Benedictine offers affordable tuition and helps students find financial aid. The Benedictine motto of "living life in balance" helps to foster friendships and relationships that can span a lifetime.

Benedictine is a part of greater Chicago's business life. Internships and excellent employment opportunities are available at several area corporations in the "Research Corridor" along I-88, which includes many Fortune 500 companies.

The University's 108-acre campus features a comprehensive learning center with a full media library and a modern and technically advanced science facility, two administrative buildings, three residence halls, Founders' Woods apartments, an athletic center, a small lake, a student center, and the newly opened sports complex, featuring a lighted multi-purpose football/soccer stadium with a nine-lane track and lighted baseball and softball fields.

Benedictine believes education is a lifelong process, not something that just happens during the college years. Class sizes are small (the student-to-teacher ratio is 14-to-1), so professors can get to know each student and learn their strengths and weaknesses. Benedictine graduates are accepted into some of the most prestigious graduate programs in the country.

The Great Issues-Great Ideas lecture series at Benedictine offers students the chance to meet world leaders. An impressive array of speakers have been a part of this series, including Nobel Peace Prize Laureate Archbishop Desmond Tutu, former Soviet Union President Mikhail Gorbachev, former United States President George Bush and First Lady Barbara Bush, former Secretary of State Madeleine Albright, and former Mayor of New York Rudy Giuliani.

Benedictine University and Springfield College in Illinois announced a permanent partnership in January 2003 to bring Benedictine programs and services to the Springfield area, Illinois' state capital.

Benedictine's Intercollegiate Athletic Program is proud to compete at the NCAA Division III level as a member of the Northern Illinois-Iowa Conference and the Illini-Badger Football Conference. The philosophy of Benedictine athletics revolves around the firm belief that "winners graduate." The "student" in student-athlete is always the highest priority.

Benedictine University dedicates itself to the education of undergraduate and graduate students from diverse ethnic, racial and religious backgrounds. As an academic community committed to liberal arts and professional education —

distinguished and guided by its Roman Catholic tradition and Benedictine heritage — the University prepares its students for a lifetime as active, informed and responsible citizens and leaders in the world community.

Benedictine University is a Catholic university in the Benedictine tradition that provides a values-centered liberal arts education enriched by our excellence in science.

Benedictine University
5700 College Road
Lisle, IL 60532-0900
630.829.6000
www.ben.edu

Benedictine University: Informing today — Transforming tomorrow

The student population at Benedictine University is a blend of people from diverse ethnic, racial and religious backgrounds, which enhances the school's cultural climate.

Benedictine University sits on a beautiful campus in Lisle, Illinois. The 108-acre campus features a comprehensive learning center, administrative buildings, three residence halls, Founders' Woods apartments, an athletic center, a small lake, a student center and a new sports complex.

As College of DuPage recognizes Naperville's 175 years of remarkable progress, it will also celebrate two other milestones. The first is the 40th anniversary of the Illinois Public Community College Act of 1965; the second, passage of a local referendum on Dec. 4, 1965, that created College of DuPage. These initiatives resulted in a partnership between college and community as solid as the city's wooden bridges spanning the DuPage River.

The tradition of excellence that has bonded C.O.D. and Naperville can be traced to 1966 when Dr. Dale M. Lipe, a Naperville resident and orthodontist, won election to the college's charter Board of Trustees. His campaign was aided by his advocacy for the 1965 referendum that called for a community college to serve Naperville and all the communities comprising District 502.

History also records that when C.O.D. first opened on Sept. 25, 1967, its administrative offices were headquartered in Naperville on Ferry Road in the old Northern Illinois Gas building.

The city's tradition of providing enlightened leadership for its community college continued in the 1970s and 1980s as Naperville's

James J. Blaha and James E. Rowoldt each held the gavel as chairman of C.O.D.'s governing Board. The college's longest-serving president, Dr. Harold D. McAninch, who transformed C.O.D. into a nationally renowned institution during his tenure from 1979 to 1994, is also a long-time Naperville resident.

Personifying Naperville's spirit of volunteerism are James Blaha, Principal, FOCUS Capital Advisors of Downers Grove, and Michael C. Brown, Vice President, Gilbane Building Co., of Chicago, city residents serving on today's C.O.D. Foundation Board.

Over the past 20 years, Naperville residents enrolled at C.O.D. — approximately 4,000 each academic

term — have led those from any of the other 50 communities served by the college. C.O.D. is proud that among them were Mayor A. George Pradel and sons George, Jr., and Gary, each of whom earned associate's degrees at the college.

As Naperville and C.O.D. celebrate their pasts, an even more exciting future awaits. Symbolic of the college's commitment to serving the city are plans to nearly double the size of its Naperville Center at 1223 Rickert Drive. This true neighborhood facility offers an array of courses applicable to the college's seven associate's degrees and the 90 certificates and degrees for occupational and technology careers.

In 2005, College of DuPage celebrates the 40th anniversary of legislation that enabled it to provide outstanding educational opportunities for the entire Naperville region.

The Naperville Center addition will feature anatomy, physiology and integrated engineering labs; enhanced classrooms; and a Center for Independent Learning. It will offer hundreds of credit and non-credit courses, including an Adult Fast Track program for busy working adults. C.O.D. is also exploring partnerships with Naperville Districts 203 and 204 that will enhance programs meeting the expectations of Naperville residents, no matter their academic need.

Also on the horizon are projects outlined in C.O.D.'s Facilities Master Plan that include Glen Ellyn campus renovations and new centers for Health Careers, Sciences, Early Childhood Education and Technology Education.

Through its Business and Professional Institute, the college links Naperville's business and industry with a myriad of educational and training opportunities. BPI's Healthcare Education Institute has entered into a visionary partnership with the Illinois Hospital Research and Educational Foundation, a subsidiary foundation of the Naperville-based Illinois Hospital Association. The partnership will expand clinical and non-clinical education for Illinois health care professionals.

Embraced by a community that values higher education, College of DuPage takes pride in continuing its legacy as Naperville's partner in progress.

College of DuPage
425 Fawell Boulevard
Glen Ellyn, Illinois 60137-6599
630.942.2380
www.cod.edu

College of DuPage's Naperville Center is a true neighborhood facility offering an array of courses applicable to the college's seven associate's degrees and the 90 certificates and degrees for occupational and technology careers. Plans are in the works to nearly double the center's current size.

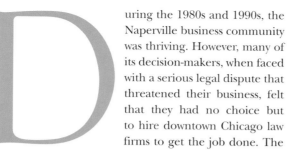

During the 1980s and 1990s, the Naperville business community was thriving. However, many of its decision-makers, when faced with a serious legal dispute that threatened their business, felt that they had no choice but to hire downtown Chicago law firms to get the job done. The Collins Law Firm, founded by Shawn Collins in August 1993, was formed to prove that the highest-caliber litigation services were available right here in Naperville.

Since its founding, The Collins Law Firm has routinely produced terrific legal results for its mostly small and medium-sized business clients. In fact, the Firm has done its best work in high-stakes cases, where its clients needed to win, or go out of business. What's more, the Firm has undertaken the rare practice of handling many such cases on a "contingent fee" basis, where its clients need not pay unless and until the Firm produces positive results.

The Firm has also aggressively represented area families whose environment has been threatened by pollution. Since 2000, the Firm has brought lawsuits against polluters whose environmental misconduct has contaminated thousands of family properties in the western suburbs of Chicago. In these Federal court cases, through the Firm's efforts, these families have recovered millions of dollars to restore clean water and lost property value.

Unlike most firms, The Collins Law Firm does litigation exclusively. This has allowed the Firm to focus all its energies on top-flight courtroom work and on producing excellent results where clients need it most.

The goal of The Collins Law Firm is no different today than it was on the day it was founded: to challenge ourselves each and every day to be one of the very best law firms in Illinois, if not the country. And we are very proud to be doing it right here in Naperville.

The Collins Law Firm
1770 North Park Street, Suite 200
Naperville, IL 60563
630-527-1595
www.collinslaw.com

Pictured from left to right: Robert L. Dawidiuk, Aaron W. Rapier, Yvonne Blackwell, Shawn M. Collins, Nancy Herron, Edward J. Manzke, Daniel C. Fabbri, David J. Fish, Ruta Norkus

MinuteMan Press of Naperville is celebrating 25 years of doing what they do best: providing the community with superior service and a true commitment to excellence. MinuteMan has developed strong roots in Naperville and surrounding communities by offering premier-quality print jobs and first-rate customer service. MinuteMan prides itself on giving back to the community and area organizations with numerous contributions and countless hours of volunteer time.

With nearly 40 employees who all live in and around Naperville, MinuteMan Press is deeply committed to one of the best cities in which to live and work. The founding partners of MinuteMan Press all grew up in this illustrious community and have decided to remain here to raise their families. John Lehman and Ray Kinney both attended Naperville Central High School, while Kevin Brahler attended the neighboring Naperville North High School.

The dedication and experience that MinuteMan employees have for their work enables them to take ownership of clients' projects with a confidence and capability that makes them famous for customer service and top-quality results.

MinuteMan's dedicated, professional staff and state-of-the-art equipment can handle all of your commercial printing and copying needs. From design to fulfillment, MinuteMan will help you make the right decision and ensure a quality product that will make you proud!

MinuteMan Press of Naperville proudly also offers copying and duplication, graphic design, promotional products and a great deal more.

MinuteMan Press is proud to always be on the leading edge of technology. MinuteMan understands that an investment in technology can actually save clients money by improving efficiencies. As a result, MinuteMan has created M2P Digital. For more information, please visit www.m2pdigital.com.

MinuteMan is located at 1577 Naperville/Wheaton Road in Naperville, Illinois. MinuteMan also shares an office in the Main Street Promenade with its sister marketing company, Maclyn Group (www.maclyngroup.com). For more information on the company and its services, please visit www.m2pnaper.com.

MinuteMan Press
1577 Naperville/Wheaton Road
Naperville, IL 60563
630.369.1360
www.m2pnaper.com

Partners Ray Kinney (left) and Kevin Brahler provide the community with superior service and true commitment to excellence. MinuteMan's machines, built with top-of-the-line technology, produce unsurpassed results for Naperville and the surrounding areas, giving MinuteMan Press its prestigious reputation.

MOSER ENTERPRISES, INC.

Moser Enterprises, Inc. was founded on July 1, 1941, as Moser Fuel and Supply by Harold Moser. During the war years, Harold and his two employees competed for Naperville's coal business.

The end of World War II signaled a new era for economic growth and prosperity in America. It was also the beginning of the end of the use of coal for heat, as more and more people switched to cleaner and more efficient fuels. Rather than switch to the fuel oil business, Harold chose an alternate approach to servicing the needs of an expanding population. In 1946, Moser Fuel and Supply become Moser Lumber, Inc.

Moser's was the third lumber yard in Naperville. There were two builders and no long-range development plans. Harold decided to create his own market, and in 1949 he bought a small farm adjacent to the city limits, developed 51 lots, and built and sold FHA homes. That was the beginning of a career built on the quality-of-life-oriented approach to development that has made Naperville one of the most desirable communities in Chicagoland. Literally dozens of builders have gotten their start on Moser-developed land.

The lumber yard benefited from this growth, but Moser's insistence on quality resulted in Moser Lumber's expansion well beyond the city limits of Naperville. During the fifties, sixties and early seventies, the majority of Moser's business was done outside of Naperville. In 1963 Moser built a new office/home center complex. The home center was one of the first of its kind in the nation and resulted in a larger commitment to the growing "do-it-yourself" trade.

Moser Lumber changed hands in 1969. Jim Moser had worked for Harold since 1943. Beginning on a part-time basis, he worked in the yard and made deliveries in Moser's one truck. After graduation from St. Norbert College and service as a lieutenant in the U.S. Army, Jim rejoined Harold on a full-time basis, first as an outside salesman calling on contractors, then as a sales manager. In 1997, Moser Lumber, Inc. merged with its sister company, Moser Enterprises, Inc., and soon thereafter discontinued the lumber business to concentrate on land development.

Moser Enterprises' growth is due to more than serendipitous circumstance. According to Jim Moser, "We subscribe to the popular quote, 'The past is prologue.' We'll never be content to rest on our laurels … we want to continue to grow, to move ahead, and to that end, Moser has a master plan. The master plan has undergone several revisions, but the foundation remains the same.

We are dedicated to the community. We demonstrate that spirit through our participation in community events and service."

Jim has set a high standard of personal service to the community, having served as chairman of the Naperville Riverwalk Committee since its inception in Naperville's sesquicentennial year of 1981. He was a major contributor to the formation of the Riverwalk, which is one of the most unique and beautiful community assets to be found anywhere in the nation. It is a series of parks along the banks of the DuPage River, stretching from Jefferson Avenue on the west through the downtown district to Fredenhagen Park and beyond on the east.

On August 31, 1998, with the passing of James Moser, the company entered into a new phase of growth via a viable Estate Plan. The company's operations are managed by a highly professional management group overseen by an active Board of Directors. This Board consists of family members, trustees who are non-family members, and senior Moser Enterprises executives. This talented group, committed to the perpetuation of the "legacy of James Moser," is very actively involved in numerous land acquisitions, developments and communities expanding far into the next generations.

> *"The legacy lives on."*

Moser Enterprises, Inc.
300 East 5th Avenue, Suite 430
Naperville, IL 60563
(630) 420-3000
Fax (630) 420-8930
www.moserenterprises.com

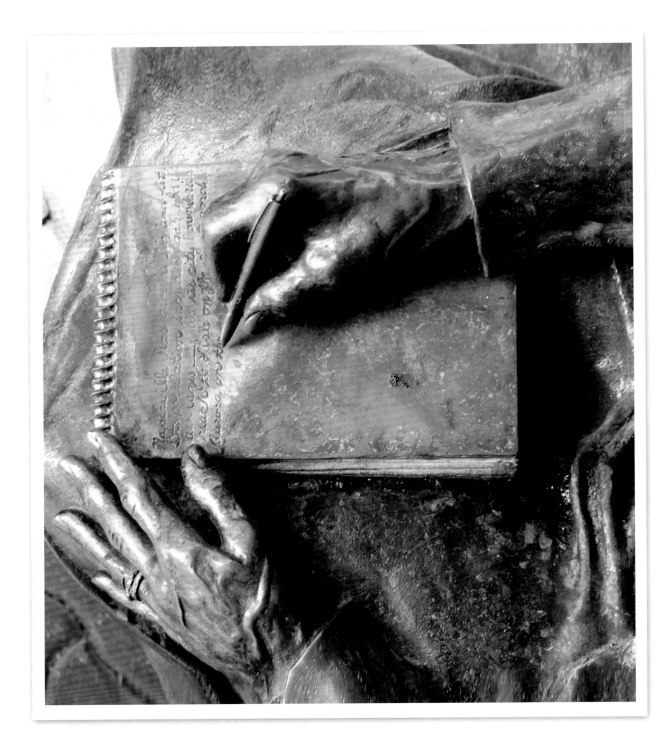

MAKING AN

On the heels of the city's recognition as one of the best places to raise a family in America, Naperville residents sometimes find it's tough to be modest when organizations suddenly honor their hometown for its good looks, good books and family appeal.

From the Riverwalk, Fredenhagen Park, the public library, Naper Settlement and local festivals to math programs, music programs and championship teams at local schools, the community has earned its share of bragging rights.

Naperville has been recognized for some of its finest assets. For instance, after becoming the winning entry in the 2004 America in Bloom national beautification competition, Naperville once again poised itself to impress the judges internationally in the 2005 Communities in Bloom program.

The Communities in Bloom beautification program is affiliated with America in Bloom and provides information and education about beautifying and preserving the environment. The international annual awards program recognizes cities all over the world for their achievement in floral displays, landscapes, turf, urban forestry, community involvement, heritage conservation, environmental awareness and tidiness. And Naperville is among them.

New initiatives and fund-raising events on the horizon ignite activism and volunteerism, giving residents leadership opportunities to work together in the spirit of cooperation to enhance the quality of life.

Our personal responsibility and community partnerships provide ways to benefit all concerned.

Pioneers from Joe Naper's days set examples for future visionaries to step up and keep progress moving forward. Earthwork around town paves the way for new development. Redevelopment is around every corner. New ideas are boundless, as dreams are turned into reality.

The combined efforts of the City, Naperville Park District and the school districts, as well as many other community organizations and individual residents, lead the way to success.

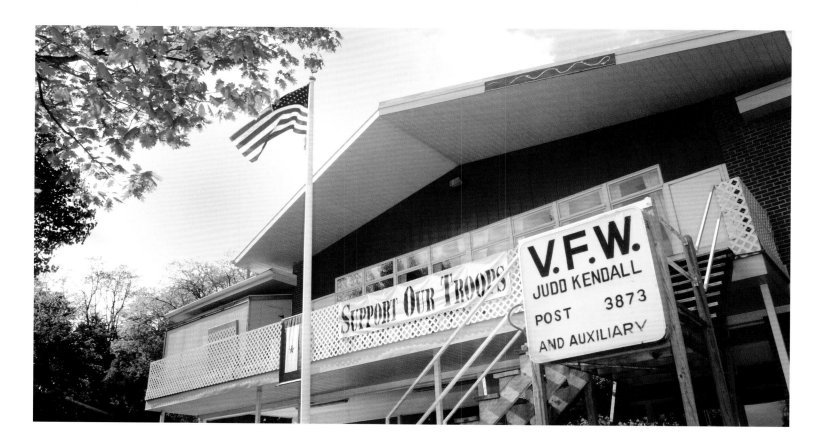

Pausing to reflect on

175 years is a good thing.

Who will be the next mayor?

What's the next step?

When will we

achieve build-out?

Where do we want to be

when the **community**

celebrates its

200th anniversary?

How does a community

best **ensure that future**

generations participate

and rejoice in the

accomplishments

of their hometown?

Leadership comes in all shapes and sizes and areas of expertise to keep Naperville vibrant and looking toward the future. Members of service clubs, homemakers and business executives volunteer together, bringing much diversity of thought and creativity to the table.

City councilmen, school board members and park district commissioners, as well as members of the Naperville Area Chamber of Commerce, Naperville Heritage Society, Naperville Development Partnership, Riverwalk Commission, Riverwalk Foundation, Century Walk, Naperville Municipal Band, DuPage Children's Museum, Millennium Carillon Foundation and United Way agencies — just to name a few — welcome input from the community at large as they assess the cultural amenities, human care needs and business climate that attract residents and visitors to Naperville.

Former Mayor Chet Rybicki

Photo courtesy of Stephanie Penick

Exemplary **community**

pride and **patriotism**

are at the **heart** of many

community **events**.

Photo courtesy of Stephanie Penick

Photo courtesy of Stephanie Penick

Photo courtesy of Stephanie Penick

Every gala, every ceremony, every dinner and every **special event** is carefully planned. Hundreds of citizens **volunteer together** for months on end in **support** of worthwhile projects and local charities. The **strong community** network **welcomes** everyone and connects citizens in a wide range of participation — often before the business day begins and way into the after hours.

Sometimes graduates who make their way in the world return home to share experiences of their travels. For instance, World Trade Ambassador Robert B. Zoellick, Naperville Central High School Class of 1971, has served under three U.S. Presidents: Ronald Reagan, George H. W. Bush and George W. Bush. The Naperville Area Chamber of Commerce hosted a "meet and greet" reception for the trade policy advisor in September 2003. Before Zoellick addressed an audience in City Council Chambers, he led a round-table discussion in the Mayor's Conference Room for selected high school government students.

Fredenhagen Park is dedicated to the memory of Grace Towsley and Walter S. Fredenhagen, who married and together helped build Prince Castles and Cock Robin Ice Cream Companies, a thriving enterprise from 1931 to 2000.

Situated on property gifted to the city by the couple's children, Rita Harvard and Ted Fredenhagen, the gateway park recognizes civic-minded generosity. The Fredenhagen Family has significantly impacted the early development of Naper Settlement and Edward Hospital, as well as many other community endeavors.

The "Two in a Million" sculpture depicts likenesses of Grace and Walter Fredenhagen for Century Walk, an outdoor public art exhibit featuring prominent people, places and events of the 20th century.

Naperville city government offices made the rounds from a location on Jefferson Avenue to another on Jackson Avenue before the Naperville Municipal Center was built and dedicated in 1992, when Mayor Sam Macrane was in office. Today, the Municipal Center is home to the offices of the mayor, city council and many other city departments.

Money magazine ranked Naperville as the third most desirable place to live in the United States in July 2005. Other groups have also honored Naperville as one of the top communities in the nation to raise children, walk, retire or start a home-based business.

The city boasts nationally acclaimed schools, the best public library system in the country for six years in a row, a remarkably low crime rate for a city of its size, and some of the most beautiful gardens and landscaping anywhere in the world.

The Naperville Woman's Club has been dedicated to service and philanthropy since 1897. Monthly meetings are held in the organization's clubhouse, located in a historic church building at 14 South Washington Street.

James L. Nichols, known as Naperville's first philanthropist, was a professor at North Central College who also wrote one of America's best-selling books, *The Business Guide.* When he died, he left $10,000 to establish the city's public library, which bears his name. The former Nichols Library, now the home for two churches, stands at 110 North Washington Street.

Even a century ago, businesses were promoted for taking an active role in supporting the local economy.

This vintage 1-cent postcard, postmarked June 10, 1909, depicts Naperville about 100 years ago. The buildings shown include the campus of North Central College, Edward Sanitarium, Kroehler Manufacturing, Old Nichols Library and the Naperville Academy.

Harris is a full-service financial institution with 170 branch locations throughout Chicagoland, including six convenient locations in Naperville along with locations in the surrounding suburbs of Lisle, Wheaton and Aurora. We offer consumer, commercial, real estate and cash-management products, as well as wealth-management services such as private banking, investment management and trust.

BACKGROUND

N. W. Harris came to Chicago in the late 1800s to help America expand westward. In 1882, he founded what has become Harris on the principles of honesty and fair dealing — principles we believe in to this day.

Harris has had a physical presence in the Naperville community since 1957. We employ over 6,000 employees in Chicagoland; approximately 100 of those are in the Naperville offices.

SERVICES

Harris' Personal Financial Services include checking and savings; money market accounts and certificates of deposit; mortgages, loans and lines of credit; retirement planning and investments; card services; and online services.

Business Banking services include business checking and savings, business loans and credit cards, merchant services, cash management, retirement planning and investments, and online services. Where appropriate, we also offer financing solutions, wealth management and employee benefits, as well as international services.

Private Banking and Investing Services employ tailored banking solutions to address the accumulation, protection and growth of our customers' money.

OUR CUSTOMERS

Our customers are the individuals, businesses and other organizations that comprise our community. Whether it is a child opening his or her first savings account or an individual planning retirement, we have the products and services to meet their needs.

Our business customers also reflect the full spectrum from startup to mature business, and we are fully equipped to meet their diverse needs.

COMMUNITY PRIDE

As a community bank, Harris is focused on the broad-based needs of individuals and businesses in the greater Naperville area.

We are actively involved in many local organizations, and you will see us represented at a variety of civic and charitable events. Our employees volunteer throughout the community, and you'll find Harris supporting the cultural and educational projects that make Naperville special.

Harris N.A.
503 N. Washington Street
Naperville, IL 60563
630.420.3500
www.HarrisBank.com

Harris has six convenient locations in Naperville, ready to serve all your financial needs, whether personal or business. Visit us today to learn more about our many banking and investment services.

B P America Inc., a key part of BP, is a major producer and manufacturer of energy and petrochemicals, with a commitment to performance, the environment and innovation.

BP IS ONE OF THE WORLD'S LARGEST OIL AND GAS COMPANIES, with operations in 100 countries and more than 100,000 employees worldwide.

Following the merger of British Petroleum and Amoco in 1998 and BP acquisitions of ARCO, Burman Castrol, and Vastar a year later, the company became the largest producer of oil and gas in North America. In July 2000, the company unveiled the Helios logo, a symbol of BP leadership in energy in all its forms coupled with an abiding concern for the environment.

BP America Inc., headquartered in Warrenville, has operations in nearly every state and more than 40,000 employees across the nation. Its businesses include the exploration and production of oil and natural gas and the refining and manufacturing of these materials into a variety of vital transportation and heating fuels; the production of a range of useful and important chemicals found in thousands of everyday products; and the safe transportation, distribution, and marketing of the fuels and lubricants that keep the engine of economy running smoothly.

Across the country, BP markets its products to motorists through more than 15,000 retail sites under the BP, Amoco and Arco brands. It also markets directly to large government, public transit, and private fleets and provides fuels and lubricants to a wide variety of industries. BP is also the leading supplier of first-fill motor fuel to the nation's automakers.

With nearly 5,000 employees in Chicagoland, BP maintains a major corporate presence in the area. The BP Leader awards annually recognize leading area nonprofit organizations in the fields of environment and education. BP employees also volunteer thousands of hours in support of community events and organizations.

As BP continues to roll out its new look to BP and Amoco sites, it also is building the "station of the future" on street corners throughout greater Chicago and other cities around the world.

"BP Connect" is the company's state-of-the-art retail station concept that places the emphasis on motorist convenience and customer taste. Inside the bright new store, fresh sandwiches, pastries and delicious unique coffees are offered at the Wild Bean Café. For now and into the future, BP is an energy company that is going "Beyond Petroleum."

BP America
150 West Warrenville Road
Naperville, Illinois 60563
877.701.2726
www.bp.com

With nearly 5,000 employees in Chicagoland, BP maintains a major corporate presence in the area.

BP's Naperville facilities are located on a beautifully landscaped, waterside campus.

W. Brand &
Mary Ann Bobosky
948 Anne Road
Naperville, Illinois 60540
630.357.1234
mbobosky@aol.com
wenotme.us

Brand and Mary Ann Bobosky caught the "bug to give back" years ago and set out to contribute to their hometown in a way that would exemplify Naperville's community spirit. Mary Ann, a seventh-generation native, and Brand are lifelong residents of the Naperville area.

Fulfilling their determination to give back, both Mary Ann and Brand have served in many leadership roles in our community. Both have served as chair of the Naperville Area Chamber of Commerce, and both have been on the board of Little Friends School. Brand has served as president of the Rotary Club of Naperville and as president of the Naperville Jaycees and is a member of the Alumni Association of Benedictine University.

Mary Ann has served as President of the Rotary Club of Naperville/Sunrise and works closely with the Naperville Initiative Committee for the DuPage Children's Museum. Mary Ann is also a member of the Naperville Branch of the AAUW and serves as vice president of the DuPage County Fair Authority. She is a member of the President's Advisory Council at Benedictine University and has served on the board of the Naperville United Way and as co-chair of the Naperville United Way Campaign.

Professionally, Mary Ann was a member of the staff of Naperville Community Unit School District 203 for over 35 years, serving in the roles of teacher, guidance counselor and administrator. Currently she is president and CEO of Advocates Building Communities Inc. and executive vice president of the Carriage Club of Naperville.

Nicknamed "Naperville's Idea Man," Brand Bobosky has spearheaded many Naperville initiatives. Thirty years ago he and Mary Ann conceptualized the extremely successful Little Friends Inc. Auction, which annually raises over $100,000 to support a variety of programs for individuals with disabilities. He was instrumental in bringing the Rotary Club of Naperville's annual Oktoberfest to the community. Most recently, he introduced and promoted Century Walk, the creation of public art throughout Naperville's

greater downtown, permanently portraying Naperville's significant 20th-century people, places and events. He is presently serving as president of Century Walk Corporation and We Not Me, Ltd.

Brand's law office is conveniently located at the corner of Chicago Avenue and Main Street, at the heart of the Riverwalk. He concentrates on commercial and residential real estate transactions, business and commercial law, estate planning and wills.

Brand and Mary Ann are members of Saints Peter and Paul Catholic Church. Parents of four and grandparents of eight, they have never lost the volunteer "bug" and are extremely proud to call Naperville home. In a "we world" they look forward to serving their community, church, family and friends for many years to come.

Brand and Mary Ann Bobosky pose by the "A Lifetime Together" sculpture of the Century Walk, donated by John Scherer, of Lakewood, Colorado, honoring his parents who grew up here, never forgetting their roots.

Anderson's Bookshop
123 West Jefferson
Naperville, IL 60540
630-355-BOOK
andersonsbookshop.com

Anderson's Bookshop
5112 North Main Street
Downers Grove, IL 60515
630-963-BOOK

W.W. Wickel Bookfair Co.
520 North Exchange Ct.
Aurora, IL 60504
630-820-0044

Oswald's Pharmacy
88 West Gartner Road
Naperville, IL 60540
630-355-2500

[Top] Anderson's Bookshop is an ideal stop for books, toys, gifts and one-of-a-kind literary events.

[Bottom] Oswald's Pharmacy moved to its current location in Naperville Plaza in 2004 and now offers medical equipment and gifts alongside its pharmacy products.

ANDERSON'S BOOKSHOP & OSWALD'S PHARMACY — GREAT SERVICE, FROM OUR FAMILY TO YOURS.

The Anderson family has a long and happy history of serving the people of Naperville. In the 130 years since an Anderson ancestor first established a business in Naperville, a warm and thriving relationship has been built between the Anderson family and the families of this city. Through Anderson's Bookshop and Oswald's Pharmacy, the Anderson family — with the sixth generation working in the stores — is proud to serve its clients and friends in the spirit of family that has made both businesses true Naperville success stories. Anderson's won the Illinois Family Business of the Year award in 2001.

Their history dates back to when W. W. Wickel started a pharmacy in Naperville. At the time, Naperville was a small farming town, so Wickel sold books along with all of the other items in the store. As Naperville grew, Wickel's grandson-in-law, Harold Kester, opened the first official bookstore above the drugstore in 1964, calling it Paperback Paradise. Since then the book part of the business has expanded and moved several times, opening two other stores and a children's wholesale bookfair company named after W. W. Wickel. Each generation of the family has added their touches and ideas to keep the stores innovative, fresh and exciting.

ANDERSON'S BOOKSHOPS

Anderson's is well-renowned for its personal service and book knowledge. Their slogan, "We sell books the old-fashioned way — we read them," is taken very seriously. Part of their mission statement is: Sharing a passion and knowledge for books to create lifelong readers.

Anderson's hosts many authors and events every year, including the "Anderson's Live Program," bringing the best of the literary world to Naperville, its community and schools. Publishers have considered Anderson's one of the best venues in the nation for their authors. Many first-time authors received their first jumpstart because of the support from Anderson's Bookshops. In 1998 an unknown author named J.K. Rowling made one of her first appearances at Anderson's with a book titled, "Harry Potter and the Sorcerer's Stone." She came back two years later attracting over 3,000 booklovers.

Anderson's has partnered with Naperville Public Libraries and School Districts 203 and 204 to create the "Naperville Reads Program," a yearly community-based reading initiative in which the entire city of Naperville is united in the joys of reading. The initiative grows every year and is reaching outside of the Naperville area. The program is unique in that the authors who are featured come to Naperville to do school and public appearances.

A commitment to community and the literary arts is what keeps Anderson's Bookshops and W. W. Wickel Co. a vital and thriving part of Naperville's past, present and future.

> **Anderson's won the Illinois Family Business of the Year award in 2001.**

OSWALD'S PHARMACY

Oswald's Pharmacy has been in continuous operation in Naperville since 1875. The store operated for 129 years at 39 W. Jefferson Ave. in the heart of downtown; in 2004 it was relocated to 88 W. Gartner Road. The store has been owned and operated by the same family for six generations.

W. W. Wickel, the original proprietor, operated the store until 1915. The store sold everything from patent medicines to farm and livestock supplies and from wallpaper to books. When "Doc Wickel" retired in 1915 he sold his store to his son-in-law, Louis Oswald, who renamed the store with the name it still bears today. Oswald guided the store through the Great Depression and two World Wars. In 1917 he added a twist that was becoming popular in drugstores around the country — a soda fountain. In 1919 the store became a Rexall-affiliated shop, a relationship that lasted into the 1970s.

In 1930, Harold Kester began to work for Louis Oswald. He soon married Oswald's daughter, Helen, and began a career that would last 70 years. When Oswald retired in 1953, Kester immediately began improving on what was already Naperville's leading drugstore. In 1960 he doubled the size of the store and did so again in 1968. These changes helped the store fend off competition as chain stores began to populate the suburbs.

Kester's son-in-law, Bob Anderson, began working at the store in 1960. Anderson bought the store from Kester in 1977 and proceeded to make improvements that kept the shop Naperville's premier pharmacy. He computerized the pharmacy in 1979; Oswald's was one of the first pharmacies in the county to do so.

In 1991, Anderson sold the store to his children, Tres Anderson, Bill Anderson, Becky Anderson Wilkins and Pete Anderson, and they continued to add to a legacy that had been in place for over a century. By 2000, downtown Naperville had become a thriving shopping and dining district. Parking and traffic congestion in this fabulously popular area began to squeeze service-oriented businesses, such as grocers and service stations, to other areas of the city. In 2004 the Anderson family decided that, to be able to continue to serve their customers into the future, a move to a more convenient location was necessary. On July 24, 2004, Oswald's opened in its current location in Naperville Plaza. The store is about 30 percent larger than Oswald's old location and has expanded to offer medical equipment as well as gift, toy and book sections.

The Anderson family still prides itself on being able to give personal attention to each customer at what has been Naperville's premier pharmacy for 130 years.

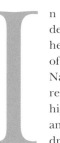

In 1845, Naperville resident Hattie Green described her new community in a letter to her parents, "We have good and the best of neighbors." Some things never change. Naperville has earned an outstanding reputation over its 175 year history. Its high quality of life, exceptional amenities and attractions, and family-friendly attitude draw more and more residents into its fold each year.

Carriage Club of Naperville is committed to Naperville's traditions of excellence. Exquisite senior living in the heart of Naperville's thriving south area helps connect our past with our present and future. Carriage Club of Naperville is an exquisite senior living community, a rare mixture of residential, cultural and historical elements assembled into a unified vision, providing a variety of living accommodations and services desired by active seniors. Carriage Club residents enjoy amenities like an art studio and wood shop, chapel, health & fitness center, library, on-site banking, regularly scheduled activities and events, and restaurant-style club dining rooms. All carriage homes and apartments include 24-hour security and emergency communications system, high-speed internet connections, and maintenance of homes and major appliances.

Carriage Club of Naperville is an exquisite new senior living community encompassing over 300,000 square feet at the intersection of 95th Street and Route 59. Amenities for the residents include fitness and wellness centers, a library, an art studio, a chapel, restaurant-style club dining rooms and various regularly scheduled activities.

Carriage Club of Naperville does everything thing it can to invite its active adult population into the community, rather than isolating them from it. We encourage our residents to explore new hobbies, cultural opportunities, and interests, both within Carriage Club itself and throughout Naperville. The Carriage Club Cultural Center will play host to events, some for residents and others for the community at-large, ranging from large holiday concerts to cozy movie nights, as well as meetings and gala affairs.

Carriage Club of Naperville is located in Naperville Crossings, a 75 acre destination experience at the crossroads of Route 59 and 95th Street. Carriage Club residents live within walking distance to shopping, dining, banking, entertainment, recreation and amenities. Naperville Crossings features pedestrian friendly walkways, a wide range of dining options, from quick snacks to romantic dinners to late night bites, independent boutique and national brand name stores, live and cinematic entertainment, and community events.

Naperville Crossings is also home to an extension of downtown Naperville's Century Walk called the Century Gardens Sculpture Walk, which features brilliant works of art by artists from across the country. Naperville history comes alive again in a 1921 Sears barn from Naperville's own Hatchwood Farm, which has been refurbished and restored to serve as an art gallery. The Dee Pasternak Memorial Garden honors the founder of the Naperville Art League, and within that, the Marjorie Meyer Memorial Fountain commemorates Naperville's farming families. A fully refurbished 1909 Homewood Glasshouse Conservatory rounds out the collection of history-turned-art, where residents can take part in cultural and horticultural activities.

> " *The place to be...*
>
> *The best of everything...*
>
> *Carriage Club*
>
> *of Naperville.* "

Since first coming to Naperville, Carriage Club has demonstrated its commitment to the community through partnerships with organizations like Naperville Community Unit School District 203, Indian Prairie School District 204, Heritage YMCA Group, Naper Settlement, Naperville Area Chamber of Commerce, Naperville United Way, North Central College, and Positively Naperville.

Back in 1845, Hattie Green was delighted with her new neighbors and her new community. Today, over 160 years later, Naperville continues to delight its long-established and newly relocated residents alike. Carriage Club of Naperville is proud to count itself among such a long list of the good and best of neighbors in Naperville.

For more information, please call (630) 753-9725 or visit www.CarriageClubOfNaperville.com.

Images courtesy of Legat Architects.

MidAmerica Bank
1001 S. Washington St.
Naperville, IL 60540
630.420.1001

1308 S. Naper Blvd.
Naperville, IL 60540
630-420-8400

3135 Book Rd.
Naperville, IL 60540
630-305-6100

9 E. Ogden Ave.
Naperville, IL 60540
630-420-8000

www.midamericabank.com

MidAmerica Bank has been dedicated to Naperville for over 30 years. In 1974, the Bank, (then MidAmerica Federal Savings and Loan), opened its first branch on Washington Street in Naperville. Over the years, three more Naperville branches have been established. These branches are located on Ogden Avenue, Book Road, and Naper Boulevard. Now with 73 offices throughout Chicago and Milwaukee, and their surrounding areas, the Bank brings the strength of over $9 billion in assets to its Naperville customers.

Over the years, the Bank has helped thousands of area citizens secure loans. These loans help them attain their dreams of owning homes, opening businesses, going to college, and much more. In addition to loans, the Bank offers its customers a full range of financial services products from savings and checking accounts to investment and retirement products.

Further cementing their relationship with Naperville, the Bank has created over 6,300 single-family homes in 23 different subdivisions through MAF Developments, a wholly-owned subsidiary of the Company. Some of the subdivisions in Naperville include Ashbury, Hobson West, and currently in development, Tall Grass of Naperville.

The Bank has also been a long-time community partner working closely with the citizens and community organizations of Naperville and the surrounding area. As a community advocate, many employees of MidAmerica Bank have served in leadership positions for various organizations in Naperville, such as the Chamber of Commerce, Edward Hospital, and the YMCA. Since 2002, MidAmerica Bank has also been an Athletic Park Partner with the Naperville Park District. Additionally, MidAmerica has created an innovative program called CommUNITY Banking that has helped many area participating non-profit organizations. Participating organizations receive donations for every new MidAmerica Bank account opened by its members. Today our community relationships continue to be one of our most prized assets.

MidAmerica Bank is proud to be part of Naperville's rich heritage and salutes the city on its 175th anniversary.

Through its subsidiary MAF Developments, MidAmerica Bank has created over 6,300 single-family homes in 23 different subdivisions, including Harmony Grove and Tall Grass.

Now with 73 offices throughout Chicago and Milwaukee and their surrounding areas, MidAmerica Bank brings the strength of over $9 billion in assets to its Naperville customers.

IT'S OUR

In sharp contrast to the small farming community where blacksmith shops, printers, stone carvers, livery stables, breweries, nurseries, sawmills and grist mills met the needs for a growing community in the 1800s, high technology and research reign at the core of Naperville's business success today.

Major area employers include Edward Hospital, in the heart of the city, as well as Lucent Technologies, Nicor Gas, BP America Inc., Tellabs and many others along Naperville's high-tech business corridor.

Calamos Investments, Laidlaw and ConAgra are among corporate leaders with headquarters in Naperville.

Through an active chamber of commerce, partnerships, local governments, boards and commissions, service organizations, special events and sponsorships, it's Naperville's business to be genuinely engaged with a generous spirit of progress at many levels.

Taking responsibility to serve the community with other businesses — from large corporations to small mom and pops — remains essential for every employer. Inclusiveness and opportunities for active participation have gone a long way toward keeping everyone headed in the same direction when it comes to the community's long-term goals and quality of life.

Naperville works because its business community volunteers and gives back to worthy causes and projects. Residents shop locally in support of the businesses that routinely sponsor their fundraisers, special events and community assets.

Naperville's success has come with knowing when to re-engineer. Large corporations downsize. Midsize businesses grow. Small businesses streamline. Though the business landscape continually changes, its commitment to the community stays the same.

Developing a great climate for business is recognizing that much of what goes into being an effective community is learned by accepting the challenges that come with change. And even with the ups and downs of uncertainty in a global economy, a positive attitude is a must.

Sometimes it appears Naperville has been blessed with a flawless touch in leadership and motivation. The truth is that folks in Naperville are willing to adapt and take risks. Folks here focus on opportunity. And they admit mistakes when they make them and overcome obstacles.

Folks in Naperville have worked, partnered,

> "Naperville's solid business plan has evolved over time to meet its growing population with an old-fashioned work ethic."

volunteered and played hard to develop these traits and assets to their utmost.

Naperville's willingness to take risks has created top-flight initiatives along the way that enhance the quality of life and, for whatever reason, has naturally and continually attracted first-rate citizens from Captain Joe Naper to today.

All signs suggest that the fourth-largest city in Illinois — with easy access to major interstate highways, O'Hare International and Midway airports, and passenger and freight railroad systems — will continue traveling on its widening path to economic success.

Mayor Margaret "Peg" Price is often credited with naming the "N Building," a distinctive landmark for suburban Naperville located along Warrenville Road in the Corporated Corrdor. The impressive office building, which appears to have an N on each of its four sides, was designed by legendary architect Helmut Jahn.

Naperville's Corporate Corri-dor is a major office and corporate head-quar-ters center that grew im-pressively in the late 20th century. In fact, ever since 1966, when AT&T located a division of Bell Labora-tories along Warrenville Road, Naperville has ex-per-ienced a period of corporate and population growth that continues today.

Over the years, Naperville has played host to many corporations that have had both **regional** and **national** markets. Today, **manufacturers** in Naperville **produce** metal, food, paper and plastic products, electrical equipment, machinery, computer parts and medical supplies.

Photo courtesy of Naperville Heritage Society

Photo courtesy of Naperville Heritage Society

Peter Kroehler, an 1892 graduate of North Central College, built Kroehler Manufacturing into what was Naperville's largest employer for most of the first half of the 20th century.

Edward Hospital and Health Services is the largest employer in Naperville, with more than 4,000 employees. In 2005, the state-of-the-art Edward Cancer Center opened to offer a full range of cancer care, from prevention and education to radiation treatment and chemotherapy, all in one place. Edward Hospital continually expands to meet the demands of the community.

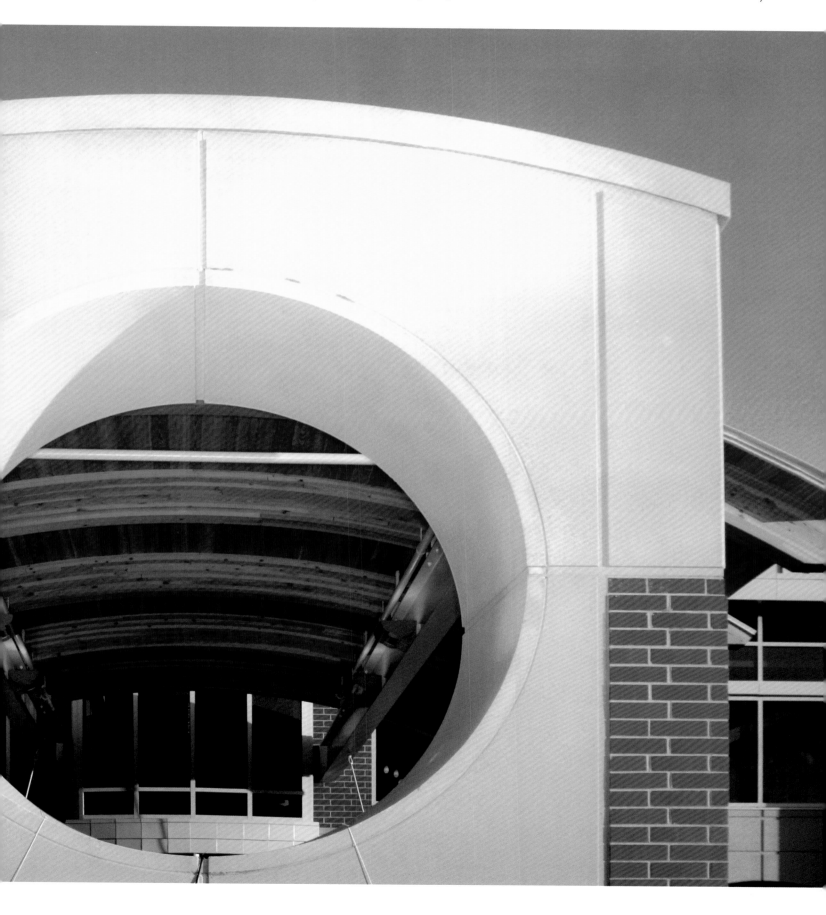

Fifth Avenue Station, an enormous warehouse and factory built for Kroehler Manufacturing Company at the turn of the 20th century, has been restored to house several restaurants, retail businesses, atrium offices, luxury lofts and apartments, as well as the School of Performing Arts.

Diners will discover local favorites, as well as many ethnic possibilities, throughout town.

Jefferson Hill Shops, comprised of a group of boutiques and a tea room, is located in the historic home, where the family of F.A. Kendall lived nearly a century ago. Kendall served as Naperville's mayor from 1913–1919.

Though Naperville continues to celebrate many firsts at 175 years, the small farming community that served as the first DuPage County seat was 33 years old before steam-powered engines puffed into town to provide local railway service. Back then, the village missed growth that settled in more progressive towns along the Chicago and Northwestern Railroad up north.

In 1864, the Chicago, Burlington and Quincy Railroad quickly led to progress and connection with other markets, but not soon enough to keep the county seat from Wheaton. In 1868, an entourage of "40 daring men" from Wheaton stole into the night to capture the county records from the courthouse in Naperville. The rest is history that comes alive in wonderful stories at Naper Settlement.

Today, the Burlington Northern Santa Fe Railway tracks are also used by AMTRAK and Metra passenger trains.

The **Main Street Promenade** includes up to 44,000 square feet of **premium retail space** and 80,000 square feet of **executive suites** in Naperville's first lifestyle center, carefully planned and designed to fit into the existing neighborhood and **downtown**. The Naperville Area Chamber of Commerce and the Downtown Naperville Alliance are located on the third level of this **active hub** for many Naperville businesses.

Naperville's corporate corridor is enhanced with the sparkling presence of Lucent Technologies, a corporate office center designed by the world-renowned architectural firm of Kevin Roche, John Dinkeloo and Associates. The Naperville building is located in front of Lucent's Indian Hill Main building, constructed for Bell Laboratories in 1968. As another note of interest, Roche was a designer of the Gateway Arch in St. Louis.

Photo courtesy of Lucent Technologies

Photo courtesy of Lucent Technologies

THE DOWNTOWN NAPERVILLE ALLIANCE

**The Downtown
Naperville Alliance**
55 S. Main Street
Suite 351
Naperville, IL
60540
630.544.3372

The Downtown
Naperville Alliance
works to promote
the city's Central
Business District not
only as a great place
to shop and dine,
but as an appeal-
ing and picturesque
destination.

The Downtown Naperville Alliance (DNA) is a non-profit organization that exists to help downtown Naperville remain a strong and vital destination for residents and non-residents alike to shop, dine and enjoy. The DNA was formed in 2001 after property owners and merchants in Naperville's central business district decided to combine efforts. Previously, these two groups had been represented by the Central Area Naperville Development Organization (CANDO) and the Downtown Merchants' Association (DMA), respectively.

In an agreement established with the City of Naperville, the DNA would be funded through a Special Service Area and the funds would be used to "promote, advertise, and pursue economic development activities on behalf of the Central Business District for the purpose of business expansion and retention." In addition, the DNA also serves as a liaison between the City of Naperville, its various departments, and the local merchants and property owners on issues that directly impact the downtown. Recent issues that have been addressed included truck deliveries in the downtown, garbage consolida-tion, parking availability, tow zones, way finding/signage, taxi and valet ordinances, and bike routes, just to name a few. The DNA also interacts with various groups offering or conducting activities in the central business district.

The Downtown Naperville Alliance is dedicated to the economic vitality and quality of life of Naperville's central business district. The organization is committed to promoting the common good of the community, communicating our

service, quality and value to customers and drawing strength, knowledge and support from each other as we continue to enhance our city.

Forces Inc.'s bright orange lightning bolt has become a familiar sight both in Naperville and around the country.

Forces Inc. is a Women's Business Enterprise that provides rental of electric generators, portable light towers, and on-site heating and air conditioning and was behind the scenes as Naperville grew from a small rural community to one of the best places to live in the United States.

The company's generators provide power for construction, events, emergencies and the fun that comes to Naperville. Forces Inc. has provided power for Naperville's Last Fling and Ribfest for more than a decade.

The company's equipment has been present for the making of award-winning movies, important political events, exciting public concerts and sports history. Forces Inc. even had a hand in wiping away the Cubs' curse: When the Bartman ball needed blowing up, Forces Inc. was there to provide the power.

Whether working to create entertainment, to build a community or to provide the emergency power to stabilize businesses and recover faster in times of crisis, Naperville leaders know they can count on Forces Inc., a company that takes pride in NOT HAVING VOICEMAIL and in providing good quality customer attention.

Forces Inc.
31W350 Diehl Road
Naperville, IL 60563
630.369.4100
(fax) 630.369.2706

"*The power is always on at Forces Inc.*"

Forces Inc.'s trucks, with their distinctive orange lightning bolt logo, are familiar sights at important events in Naperville and the surrounding communities.

City of Naperville
400 South Eagle Street
Naperville, Illinois 60566
www.naperville.il.us

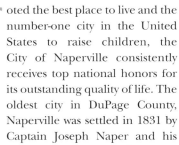

Voted the best place to live and the number-one city in the United States to raise children, the City of Naperville consistently receives top national honors for its outstanding quality of life. The oldest city in DuPage County, Naperville was settled in 1831 by Captain Joseph Naper and his brother, John. Nearly two centuries later, Naperville is now home to more than 140,000 residents, making it the fourth-largest city in Illinois.

One of the fastest-growing cities in the country, Naperville is home to several high-tech research and development companies. Located only 30 miles from downtown Chicago, a number of national and multi-national companies have built corporate headquarters within the city's borders. Also known for its quaint downtown, Naperville is home to many of Chicagoland's most popular retailers and a wide assortment of four-star and casual dining establishments. Naperville's famed Riverwalk, built to celebrate the city's 150th anniversary, attracts visitors to the downtown area year-round.

Although Naperville has seen its population nearly double each decade since 1950, it has retained its small-town atmosphere and hometown values. First and foremost, the City of Naperville is dedicated to providing the highest quality of life for its citizens and businesses.

Since 1969, the City of Naperville has operated under the council-manager form of government. The city manager is the professional chief administrator for all city operations and is appointed by the City Council. An eight-member City Council and mayor are elected at-large and hold monthly public meetings at the Naperville Municipal Center. Located in the heart of the downtown overlooking the picturesque Riverwalk, the Municipal Center houses most of the city's administrative offices.

One of the major employers in the area, the City of Naperville has more than 1,000 employees who provide essential services to the city's residents. Dedicated to providing residents with "Great Service — All the Time," city employees bring a wealth of knowledge and experience to their jobs every day.

Naperville is one of the first cities worldwide to enjoy an accredited police, fire and emergency communications department. Naperville residents are protected and served by highly trained and skilled public safety professionals.

The Naperville Fire Department's 200 men and women protect more than 146,000 people in Naperville and the surrounding unincorporated Naperville Fire Protection District. Residents are currently served by eight fire stations, with an additional two stations scheduled to be built in the near future. The Naperville Fire Department is one of only a few departments in the United States to be awarded full accreditation by the Commission on Fire Service Accreditation International.

Naperville's Office of Emergency Preparedness and Homeland Security oversees emergency and disaster planning and maintains its Outdoor Warning System and the city's Emergency Management Agency. This office works closely with other local, state and federal authorities to keep informed and up-to-date on homeland security issues.

Naperville's nationally accredited Police Department employs a staff of almost 300, whose mission is to provide professional, high-quality and effective police service in partnership with the community. Of all Illinois cities with populations greater than 100,000, Naperville has the lowest

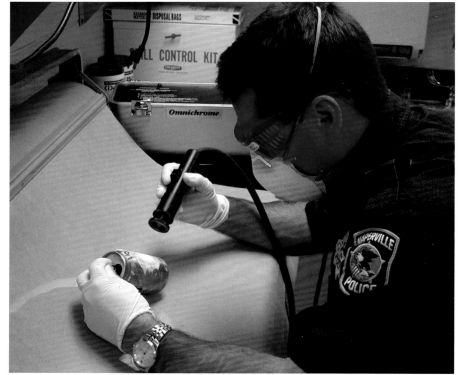

Naperville is one of the first cities worldwide to enjoy an accredited police, fire and emergency communications department. Naperville's nationally accredited Police Department employs a staff of almost 300. Housed in a state-of-the-art facility just west of downtown, Naperville Police Department personnel utilize the most advanced methods of crime prevention and investigation to maintain the community's safe neighborhoods, businesses and city streets.

crime rate and the lowest per capita cost for police services. Housed in a state-of-the-art facility just west of downtown, Naperville Police Department personnel utilize the most advanced methods of crime prevention and investigation to maintain the community's safe neighborhoods, businesses and city streets.

Naperville's municipally owned electric, water and wastewater utilities are locally controlled and managed, providing residential rates that are among the lowest in the State of Illinois. In 2005, the city launched its Renewable Energy Option, which provides all residential and commercial utility customers within Naperville the opportunity to purchase emission-free, renewable sources of electricity from natural

Located in the heart of the downtown overlooking the picturesque Riverwalk, the Municipal Center houses most of the city's administrative offices.

Naperville is an active community with a vibrant volunteer spirit. The volunteers who serve on city and community boards and commissions exemplify this spirit to the greatest degree through their outstanding community involvement. Each year, community volunteers organize and plan numerous special events that attract hundreds of thousands of visitors to the city.

In 2003, the city dedicated the Commander Dan Shanower/September 11 Memorial in memory of the 3,031 individuals who lost their lives on September 11, 2001. The memorial is located on the south side of the city's Riverwalk, adjacent to the Naperville Municipal Center. The concept for the memorial, which was named after U.S. Navy Commander and Naperville native Dan Shanower, was developed and implemented entirely by a volunteer committee.

It is this volunteer spirit, combined with Naperville's dynamic business community, thriving downtown experience and unwavering hometown values that have helped to develop Naperville into the type of city every resident is proud to call home.

sources such as wind, sun and water. Renewable energy is the fastest-growing source of electricity nationwide, and the City of Naperville's Department of Public Utilities is leading the way in promoting the benefits of these exciting technologies to Naperville's residents and businesses.

Naperville's Public Works Department maintains the city's parking lots, storm sewers, detention basins and more than 460 miles of city streets. The department also oversees snow removal, leaf and brush collection, and mosquito control efforts.

The city's Transportation, Engineering and Development (TED) Department plays a key role in helping to maintain infrastructure for Naperville's increasing population. The city's TED Department manages the city's full spectrum of engineering, transportation and development projects. The Comprehensive Transportation Plan is the policy-based document that guides the city's decision-makers in addressing transportation issues. Each year, the TED Department is charged with implementing the plan and evaluating the projects that have been completed as part of the Annual Work Program. The TED Department also works to seek innovative ways to address traffic issues to enhance the quality of life throughout the Naperville community.

Naperville boasts nationally acclaimed schools and the number-one library system in the United States. In 2003, the 95th Street Library, a state-of-the-art learning facility, opened its doors in the southwest portion of the city. Naperville is also home to a number of cultural amenities, including public art, sculptures, memorials and museums.

The Department of Public Utilities unveiled its new Electric Utility System Control Room in December 2003. The System Control Room is staffed 24 hours a day, seven days a week and monitors the city's 16 substations.

Macom Corporation
25033 W. 91st St.
Naperville, IL 60564
630.820.9700
www.macomcorp.com

Huntington, Huntington Commons, Huntington Estates, Huntington Ridge, Knolls of Huntington, Maplebrook, Maplebrook South, Moser Highlands (East and West), Olympic Terrace, Penncross Knolls, Pembroke Commons, Saddle Creek, Saybrook, South Pointe, Tamarack South, Tamarack West, Walnut Hill, Walnut Ridge and White Eagle Club.

THE EARLY YEARS

Homebuilding had been in the doldrums during the Great Depression and then during World War II, and many economists predicted a severe recession after the war ended. But Dr. Edward "Doc" Moser and son Harold believed pent-up demand for new construction would create a corresponding demand for lumber, so they purchased a coal yard on North Washington Street and gradually converted it into a lumber yard.

Harold Moser wanted to be a priest, and he wanted to help defend his country during World War II.

But a crippling illness during adolescence left those goals out of his reach. Instead, he changed the face of Naperville forever, founding The Macom Corporation, which remains a leading force as the City celebrates its 175th birthday.

Now under the leadership of Paul Lehman, Macom and its predecessor company, the original Moser Enterprises, Inc., sometimes with partners, are responsible for the development of almost half the home sites in Naperville.

Macom has been a pioneer in the residential development industry. Macom was the first to:

- Create an 18-hole residential golf course community in the Chicago area
- Donate land for schools and parks, setting the standard for future city ordinances
- Create extensive entrance gate features and landscape buffers along perimeter roads
- Create mandatory homeowners associations responsible for maintenance of community entrance gates and perimeter landscaping, thus assuring the long-term care of the "front door" for each neighborhood
- Establish and maintain architectural standards
- Incorporate sites for religious institutions

Harold Moser passed away in 2001 at the age of 87. The Naperville City Council once called him "The Father of Modern Naperville." His innovative plans to include parkway trees, parks and land for schools in new subdivisions have become the standard in most cities. The company and its predecessor have created 32 residential communities, with additional areas in the planning stages. These Naperville communities encompass more than 8,000 single-family home sites and multi-family areas containing more than 1,000 townhomes, condominiums and apartments.

Today, the list of developments Harold Moser and Macom have been involved in developing reads like a "Who's Who" of Naperville neighborhoods: Aero Estates, Ashwood Creek, Ashwood Park, Brighton Ridge, Brookdale, Brush Hill, Carriage Hill, Cedar Glen, Columbia Estates, Cress Creek Country Club, Farmington, Forest Preserve, High Meadow,

When he returned from the war, Moser's longtime friend Harold Lehman joined the lumber business as vice president. This proved to be a great decision for both men, both personally and professionally. The two Harolds married sisters — Margaret and Kathryn. Harold Lehman worked with Harold Moser until Harold Lehman retired in 1973; in 1952 he and Kathryn had a son, Paul, who started working for Macom in 1974, the day after receiving his engineering degree from the University of Illinois.

He never left Macom. Today, Paul Lehman is president and owner of Macom. A fifth-generation Napervillian, Lehman has given back to his community through service to many organizations. Paul has served a number of terms on the Board of Directors of the Naperville Area Chamber of Commerce, including serving as its president during 1981, the City's Sesquicentennial year, and currently serves on the Board of the Naperville Development Partership. Paul also served for 10 years on the Board of Directors of Edward Hospital and has served on the Boards of the Naperville Ecumenical Adult Day Care Center, Catholic Charities for DuPage and Kendall Counties, Northern Illinois Home Builders Association, and the East-West Corporate Corridor Association. Paul has served on the Board of Trustees of Benedictine University for over 20 years and also currently serves on the Board of the DuPage Community Foundation. Paul has also been an involved member of the Rotary Club of Naperville for over 30 years, serving as its president in 1980–1981.

(TOP)
The Maplebrook communities were designed by Harold Moser to be upscale neighborhoods for move-up buyers in the '60s, complete with a residents-only swimming pool.

(BOTTOM)
Cress Creek Country Club, seen here in its early stages, was the first private residential golf course community in the Chicago area.

"This wasn't the career path I envisioned for myself as a graduate engineer, but I was very fortunate to work for — and learn from — my father and Harold Moser," Lehman says. "They showed me that it is possible to be financially successful while still retaining high ethical standards and, most importantly, the need to keep your promises."

Indeed, today, area business people know that a handshake agreement with Paul Lehman is as good as a signed contract.

By the time Paul Lehman joined the company in 1974, Naperville and Macom were doing well. But in the early years, construction in Naperville started slowly. To spark lumber sales, and because he had always had an interest in construction, Harold Moser built several dozen houses, mostly on lots purchased by his father in McIntosh Highlands.

But Moser soon ran out of lots. If he was going to keep on selling lumber, he would need to start developing more lots. Moser purchased Louise Wilson's property just south of the Burlington Forest Preserve on the town's west side. He platted 52 lots and built the homes. One of his most popular floor plans, a split-level, sold for $18,500, while a three-bedroom ranch was listed at $19,500.

The development was a success, but Naperville's modern-day growth kicked into high gear in 1955 with Moser Highlands, south of McIntosh Highlands on Sam Wehrli's farm. Moser purchased the Wehrli farm and also the Von Oven Nurseries land east of Washington Street. The neighborhood, dubbed "Moser Highlands," (later East Highlands) was designed to eventually have 575 homes, a park and a school site.

Many thought that the land was too far south. Still other detractors were convinced Moser had paid way too much for the land — some $1,000 per acre.

Long before land/cash donations were a city requirement for developers, Moser donated the land for what is now Highlands School. A referendum to finance the school had failed, and the school board had no other means to pay for it. Moser realized that homes would sell better, and that the neighborhood would be a better place to live, with a school. He donated 10 acres to the school board. With the land in hand, the school board's next referendum passed and a development standard was set.

The Highlands was an innovative development in other ways, too. Moser didn't like the monotony of single-builder subdivisions, so he sold lots to numerous builders. Each home had a parkway tree, and Moser also set aside land for a park. Parkway trees and land/cash donations for parks and schools are now standard development codes in Naperville, as well as in many other towns.

The East Highlands reflected the standards of the day. Homes ran from 1,000 to 1,800 square feet and had three bedrooms and one or two bathrooms. Most had one-car attached garages; some lots were wide enough for two-car garages. Prices started at $20,000.

The Highlands did so well that Moser quickly jumped across Washington Street and bought the Fred Hoffman farm south of Edward Hospital. There, the West Highlands began in the late 1950s. Homes grew somewhat larger, while styles stayed the same. Most homes had attached, two-car garages, averaged around 2,000 square feet and sold in the low $20,000s.

The neighborhood sprouted parkway trees and carriageways — sidewalks directly next to the street. Here again, Moser donated the land for a neighborhood school — Elmwood — which opened in the fall of 1960.

Meanwhile, big things were happening for Naperville. The East-West Tollway opened in 1959. The new road would do much to bring new jobs and residents to town.

Soon, Moser moved directly south, starting what is now known as Maplebrook I. Designed to be an upscale neighborhood for aspiring move-up buyers, Maplebrook had generously proportioned split level and ranch homes, wide sidewalks, and the coup de grace — a swimming club for residents only. Electric and telephone wires were underground.

Homes sold for $21,500 to $41,000. The first house sold in 1963 to W. F. Miller, an Argonne National Laboratory physicist, and his family, who came to typify Naperville's burgeoning population of engineers and scientists.

Maplebrook ran to 75th Street, considered by the late '50s to be the furthermost point of Naperville. The town, most figured, would never extend any farther south.

But in January 1960, the town doubled in size as the city council annexed 1,596 acres, nearly all of that for Moser developments north and south of the existing city borders.

THE COUNTRY CLUB COMMUNITIES

Upscale developments appealed to Moser, especially a golf course development he saw on one of his trips to Boca Raton, Fla. Determined to introduce one to Naperville, he began the 400-acre Cress Creek Country Club north of Ogden Avenue (Route 34) on what had been the Ehrhart and Nadelhoffer farms.

To start Cress Creek, Moser formed a new company, The Macom Corporation, in partnership with a mortgage financing company. Originally the company was to be named Mo-Mac, a combination of Moser's name and that of his new partner. But the state had already chartered another company with a similar name, so they moved some letters around and

(TOP)
Although 75th Street was once thought to be the southern edge of Naperville, Macom has expanded the boundaries, even building a private swim club community in the southernmost point of Naperville, South Pointe. Stembridge Builders operated one of several models featured in the community.

(BOTTOM)
Swimming pools have always been a popular feature in many Macom communities, including the one at Cress Creek Country Club.

"Harold stressed close attention to the fundamentals of business, construction and design details to successfully complete a first-class residential community," Lehman says. "The work doesn't stop with the sale of the lot, but continues on to the creation of a neighborhood. No matter what the price level of the community we are creating, every buyer is entitled to a quality environment, designed and built correctly."

THE FINAL NAPERVILLE DEVELOPMENTS

As White Eagle approached the halfway mark in its development, Macom turned its attention to other projects, including High Meadow — the site of the 1993 Cavalcade of Homes — and Saddle Creek, both near the intersection of Book Road and 111th Street. Once again, Macom developed successful communities in an area naysayers considered too far south.

More Naperville communities have followed, including the neighborhoods of Tamarack West, Penncross Knoll, South Pointe and Tamarack South.

Although 75th Street was once thought to be the southern edge of Naperville, Macom has expanded the boundaries, even building a private swim club community in the southern-most point of Naperville, South Pointe.

Now, Macom is once again playing the role of pioneer, as the company begins development of one of the few remaining land parcels in Naperville. This 637-acre area will include Ashwood Creek, Ashwood Park and Carillon Club of Naperville. The area will include 740 single-family homes, and 370 multi-family homes, along with more than 178 acres of open space.

As Naperville has grown, so have the sizes of homes. The minimum square footage for a home in Ashwood Creek is 2,900 square feet, while Ashwood Park begins at 3,500 square feet. Homes now have four to five bedrooms, three or more bathrooms and, in many cases, three- or four-car garages. Future amenities for both Ashwood communities include a community clubhouse with multiple swimming pools, parks and paths throughout the neighborhoods. Once again, Macom has set the standard for residential living in Naperville.

"My family has been in Naperville for five generations, and I've lived in Naperville all of my life," adds Lehman. "We always strive to develop a community that residents are proud to call home, both now and for years to come."

came up with the name Macom. Before the project began, however, Moser bought out his partner.

With Cress Creek, many residents thought he had finally gone nuts. They believed the land around Cress Creek "north of the highway" was too marshy and that he paid too much for it. One of the most widely respected appraisers in the area assessed the land and told Moser it was valueless. No one, the appraiser said, would ever build this far away from town.

Undeterred, Moser laid in the golf course and platted out 612 home sites for what would be the Chicagoland area's first private residential golf course community. The glamorous $300,000 clubhouse drew raves for its spacious Walnut Room dining room, lounge and snack bar and its swimming pool and wading pool. The country club also included an 18-hole, 6,700-yard, par 72 championship golf course with five lakes adding challenges to the fairways.

The average size of the homes grew through the '70s, '80s and '90s. They sprouted libraries, sun rooms, master suites with luxury baths and three-car garages. The gracious neighborhoods designed by Macom have sweeping lawns, generous setbacks, parks, trees and curving streets.

In 1987, White Eagle Club became Macom's flagship venture. Situated west of Route 59 in both Aurora and Naperville, the neighborhood was built around another country club, this time with a course designed by golf legend Arnold Palmer. Luxury homes started at around $350,000.

Paul Lehman purchased the company in 1993 after working with Moser for 20 years and supervising the development of White Eagle Club.

(TOP)
Paul Lehman purchased Macom from Harold Moser in 1993 after working with Moser for 20 years and supervising the development of White Eagle Club. Today, Lehman continues as president and owner.

(BOTTOM)
Situated west of Route 59, White Eagle Club was built around another country club, this time with a course designed by golf legend Arnold Palmer. Harold Moser is shown with White Eagle Golf Club in the background.

Subdivisions Developed by Macom Corporation

Subdivision Listing

1. Areo Estates
2. Ashwood
3. Ashwood Creek
4. Ashwood Park
5. Brighton Ridge
6. Brookdale
7. Brush Hill
8. Carillon Club of Naperville
9. Cedar Glen
10. Columbia Estates
11. Cress Creek Country Club
12. East Highlands
13. Farmington
14. Forest Preserve
15. High Meadow
16. Huntington
17. Huntington Commons
18. Huntington Estates
19. Huntington Ridge
20. Knolls of Huntington
21. Maplebrook I, II, South
22. Naper Carnage Hill
23. Olympic Terrace
24. Pembroke Commons
25. Penncross Knoll
26. Saddle Creek
27. Saybrook
28. South Pointe
29. Tamarack South
30. Tamarack West
31. Walnut Hill
32. Walnut Ridge
33. West Highlands
34. White Eagle Club

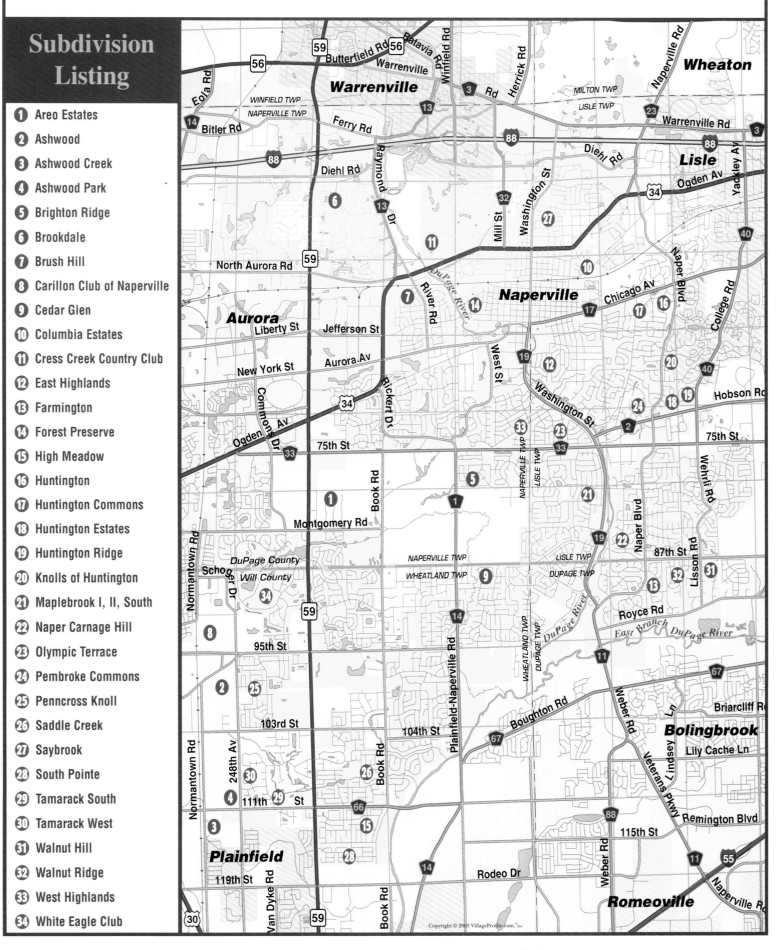

PROFILES OF

AnamArt Gallery 51

Anderson's Bookshop/Oswald's Pharmacy 125

Atwell-Hicks 48

BBM Incorporated 46

Benedictine University 99

W. Brand & Mary Ann Bobosky 124

BP America Inc. 123

Calamos Investments 74

Carriage Club of Naperville 126

William J. Carroll, Ph.D. 98

City of Naperville 144–145

College of DuPage 100

The Collins Law Firm, PC 101

The Downtown Naperville Alliance 142

Edward Hospital & Health Services 52–53

First National Bank of Naperville 77

Forces, Inc. 143

Harris N.A. 122

Holiday Inn Select 54–55

Home Improvements USA 50

Jackson Moving & Storage 73

john greene, Realtor 76

Macom Corporation 146–149

MidAmerica Bank 127

MinuteMan Press 102

Moser Enterprises, Inc. 103

Naper Settlement 75

Naperville Area Chamber of Commerce 23–25

Naperville Area Humane Society 72

Naperville Park District 49

Naperville Township 47

Nicor Gas 78–79

North Central College 94–95

School Districts 203 & 204 90

St. John's Episcopal Church 22

GOOD SOURCES ABOUT

Naperville, Illinois: 175 Years of Success is a sampler about an incredible community located just 28 miles west of Chicago's Loop.

In a few words and many pictures — photographed in time for this book to be available during the 175th Anniversary Celebration of Heritage, Unity and Vision in 2006 — we hope to provide a snapshot of the good things that set this community apart as we go forward. If this volume whets your appetite for more facts and local lore, many good books about Naperville are available in the Naperville Public Library, Naper Settlement Archival Library and local bookshops.

Special thanks to all the history buffs, photographers, artists and local writers who took the time to chronicle the lifestyles of some of Naperville's most interesting citizens, past and present.

Century Walk, a variety of outdoor art pieces in different media, depicts people, places and events of the 20th century and is located in the heart of downtown, from Naperville Central High School to North Central College, Burlington Square Park to Nichols Library, and Fredenhagen Park to Main Street Promenade. 1996 to Present.

Cowlishaw, Mary Lou. *This Band's Been Here Quite a Spell … 1859–1981.* The Naperville Municipal Band Inc., 1981.

Dale, Marilyn and Ogg, Bryan. *My Naperville Then & Now Coloring Book: Celebrating Naperville's 175th Anniversary and Riverwalk's 25th Birthday.* AnamArt Gallery, Naperville, Ill., 2005.*

Frolick, Sharon and Ruehrwein, Richard I. *Naper Settlement: A 19th Century Village.* The Creative Company, Lawrenceburg, Ind., 1999.

Fry, John. *"My Dad Says … ".* Wheatland View Publishing Inc., Naperville, Ill., 2000.

Hatch, Eldon. *Blessed My Whole Life Through.* Eldon Hatch, Naperville, Ill, 2005.

Lebeau, Pierre and Keating, Ann Durkin. *North Central College and Naperville: A Shared History.* North Central College, Naperville, Ill., 1955.

Mackenbrock, Marcia Koffron and Weber, Sharon Ridgeway. *Postmark Naperville, An A to Z History.* Enthusia Small, Naperville, Ill., 2004.*

McElroy, Kay Severinsen. *Thank You, Mr. Naperville — A Tribute to Harold Moser Upon His Retirement.* McElroy Associates Inc., Naperville, Ill., 1994.

Naper Settlement, 19th Century Living History Outdoor Museum. Accredited by the American Association of Museums. 523 South Webster Street, Naperville, Ill. 1969 to Present.

Naperville Development Partnership / Naperville Convention and Visitors Bureau. 212 South Webster, Suite 104, Naperville, Ill., 2005.

Naperville Development Partnership / Naperville Convention and Visitors Bureau. *By the Numbers 2004–2005.* Naperville, Ill., 2005.

Naperville Farmers' Riverwalk Commission. *Naperville Area Farm Families History.* Bloom Printing Corp., 1983.

Savage, Chuck. *A College and Its Community: North Central College, Naperville, Illinois, A Contemporary Photographic Portrait.* North Central College, Naperville, Ill., 2003.

Towsley, Genevieve. *A View of Historic Naperville,* fourth printing. Naperville Sun, Naperville, Ill., 1986.

Wehrli, Jean and Wehrli, Mary Lou. *The Naperville Sesquicentennial Photo Album 1831–1981.* The Naperville Sesquicentennial Commission, Naperville, Ill., 1981.

Wehrli, Joyce Elizabeth. *We Are Family: The Pre-Emption House and the Gertrude Hiltenbrand Wehrli Family.* Joyce E. Wehrli, Naperville, Ill., 1993.

*Written for children and adults

Traditionally, historians and event planners promote creating time capsules to commemorate milestones such as 175th anniversaries. Accounts and objects representative of the current period are secured in a waterproof receptacle that's placed in the ground or in a cornerstone for discovery in the future.

In these technological times, this practice can give collectors and conservators reason to pause. What's appropriate for a time capsule that might be buried for 100 years? What items will tell the story of 2006 in 2106? What natural and man-made materials will withstand the fluctuating temperatures of the Midwest?

With the vast and fast changes in technology and electronics, a CD of photos or a voice recording likely would be useless to someone 100 years from now.

When properly protected, newspapers, books and photographs last for perpetuity. Think about it. And thank goodness for the printing press.

—Stephanie Penick